20×8

That The World May Believe

Centre for
Faith and Spirituality
Loughborough University

That The World May Believe

A Parish Church moves from Renewal to Restoration

TONY HIGTON

Marshalls

Marshalls Paperbacks
Marshall Morgan & Scott
3 Beggarwood Lane, Basingstoke, Hants, RG23 7LP, UK
A subsidiary of the Zondervan Incorporation

First published in 1985 by Marshall Morgan & Scott Ltd.

British Library Cataloguing in Publication Data
Higton, Tony
    That the world may believe
    1. Pentecostalism
    I. Title
    269'.4'0924   BR1644
    ISBN 0-551-01261-7

Phototypeset by Input Typesetting Ltd, London
Reproduced, printed and bound in Great Britain by
Hazell Watson & Viney Limited,
Member of the BPCC Group,
Aylesbury, Bucks

*This book is dedicated to
my fellow members of the Body of Christ in Hawkwell
whose love and prayers have made it possible*

Contents

Preface

This book is a simple account of God's work in the Church of England parish of Hawkwell, Essex in the last ten years. It is written for those looking for a strategy for evangelism through the Body of Christ; those who feel very ordinary and inadequate in God's service; those who want to know more about the significance of charismatic renewal; those who want to lead a church on from renewal; those challenged and disturbed by the 'house-church movement' and those distressed at the moral and theological confusion in the church.

I have attempted to be honest about weaknesses and anxieties. Some aspects may prove controversial but I have tried to be constructive throughout. The book is not theory but is a description of how one ordinary congregation is seeking to work out Biblical principles, with their radical implications, within a historic denomination. The overall aim is to further our Lord's desire that the world may believe.

My thanks are due to my wife Patricia, with whom I share one ministry. Her insights, criticisms and support have been vital, both in the writing of the book and in the years it describes. I express my gratitude also to my daughter Rachel and my son Michel who are fully involved with us in the work and give constant encouragement. Finally thanks to Fiona Lindsay for demolishing my present participles; Evelyn Goldstein for proof reading, and Valerie Morris and Ruth George for typing.

1: Superficiality and Sentiment

'Where on earth is it?' we asked one another. Patricia and I were studying the map of Essex to find Hawkwell. The patrons of the living had written asking if I were interested in becoming the rector there. All we knew was that it was in Essex. After twenty minutes' scrutiny, we found it. It had literally fallen down the crack in the map! The 'Hawk' was on one page and the 'well' on the other.

We had been very happy at St. Barnabas in St. Mark's Parish, Cheltenham for nearly five years. The Lord brought us back into an experience of renewal in 1972 after four years of reacting against it. Our crisis experience of the Spirit in 1967 had been quite remarkable. It happened at a time when thousands of Christians throughout the world were experiencing the same thing, as charismatic renewal affected the historic denominations for the first time. We began to experience the 'charismatic' gifts of prophecy, healing etc. But I came across people who had been hurt by the hamfisted approach of some charismatics. There were casualties from 'healing' activities and the danger of false prophecy particularly worried me. I also found some superficiality and extremism which put me off further.

All of this coupled with lack of fellowship and teaching, made us turn away from what God had done. Consequently for my first curacy and well into my second

I was spiritually dry, having grieved the Holy Spirit by all but rejecting his work. I hit rock-bottom in 1971, realising that my life and ministry were a failure. This experience drew me closer to God, but for six months I didn't want to be associated with the 'lunatic fringe', which is how I regarded charismatics.

Eventually I gave way to the Spirit's persistence and began to attend occasional renewal meetings in the beautiful Cotswold village of Meysey Hampton. A deep yearning for the supernatural work of the Holy Spirit was stimulated in my heart. Then in April 1972 a previous curate of the parish—a convinced charismatic—made a private visit to friends in the area, and planned to hold an informal fellowship on the Saturday evening. Nobody in the church knew what was happening in me, although the Holy Spirit was beginning to work clearly in the lives of some leading members. On that Saturday morning I drove up into the hills overlooking Cheltenham to think and pray. I knew I was at a major turning point in my life. To go forward in renewal could mean facing opposition and even having to leave the parish. Previous curates had been asked to leave because of their involvement in renewal. I found the prospect very difficult but as I sat there in the weak April sunshine, I knew I could do no other than obey God. So He began to bring renewal to many in the church and we experienced great times of worship, fellowship and ministry. We became deeply attached to the people of St. Barnabas.

However, in spite of the fact that there were no great problems or excesses, opposition from people in other churches in the parish proved very painful. It had at times produced an anxiety state in me. In those times I dreaded the phone ringing or letters arriving or a car drawing up outside the house. I had a fear of disaster or of being ejected from the parish. On one occasion one

14

of my full-time colleagues rang to say we ought to leave and that the only place fit for us was the gutter. Looking back the only major mistake we made was that we were too cautious because of the opposition.

Now there was the prospect of a move. Would Hawkwell be the right place? We had no conviction about it. One showery October morning we arrived in Hawkwell and first inspected the rectory and its two and a half acres of soggy grounds. No wonder some men had turned the living down! On the other hand, what a lovely garden for our daughter Rachel, who was six and our son Michel who was three, to explore. With my strong sense of history and appreciation of beauty, I immediately fell in love with the tiny mediaeval parish church—St. Mary's. It is a picture postcard church with stone walls, a red tiled roof and a wooden spire. Inside, its ancient roof beams and stained glass windows are an attractive sight. The main east window depicts Christ ascending, and has been very helpful to me in remembering the presence of Christ. There had been 50 rectors since the year 1300. What a privilege to be the next one!

We discovered that Hawkwell is a parish of some 10,000 people. It consists mainly of estates of small private housing with many young families and elderly folk. As it is some 38 miles from London, many people commute to work in the City. The parish is in two quite distinct areas, rather like a figure of 8. Emmanuel Church is in one half. St. Mary's and the rectory are in the belt of countryside between the two areas. In the evening we met the churchwardens, who questioned us closely about renewal in general and speaking in tongues in particular. Later we drove off into the night, still not convinced Hawkwell was right for us but worried that we might have seemed too charismatic.

Over the next few days the conviction grew that we should accept the living if everyone agreed. So it was that on the frosty evening of February 6th 1975 I was instituted and inducted as rector of Hawkwell. I was determined that little St. Mary's should not be neglected in favour of the larger and more convenient modern Church of Emmanuel. So we had the first part of the service in St. Mary's which was packed to the doors. There was so little room that I remember kneeling before the bishop and having to lean back so that my nose didn't press into his stomach! Then we all—bishop, archdeacon, rural dean and I, fully robed—rushed by coach up to Emmanuel for the second half of the service. That was a good story for diocesan gossip for months afterwards!

I was determined to bring reconciliation to the parish. There was bad feeling between the two churches. St. Mary's was playing second fiddle to Emmanuel and some at Emmanuel even thought St. Mary's should be closed. In my naivety I thought I could succeed with people my predecessor had found difficult. I felt too that by diplomacy I could reconcile the 'non-charismatics' with the small group of despised charismatics. All of this seemed a laudable aim but it was really covering up my fear of being rejected. A few days before the Institution, I had met a church member in Emmanuel. 'My husband isn't very popular,' she said, 'he always speaks his mind. You just have to accept him as he is.' This caused a sinking feeling in my stomach—the sort of anxiety I had often felt in Cheltenham.

The small group of charismatics in the parish met each week, but had largely been taken over by an independent group from outside the church. I didn't feel entirely at home in that fellowship. One of the churchwardens urged me to close it down, but I had other ideas. A visit to Southend by Trevor Dearing gave me an opportunity to speak about my mixed experience of renewal and particularly of the various good things I had discovered.

16

'The dominant themes in the charismatic movement at present,' I wrote, 'are praise and adoration to God, the lordship of Christ over the whole of life, complete obedient openness to the Holy Spirit, loving and honest fellowship between Christians, the discovery of the ministry of every Christian in the Body of Christ, submission to authority, and the healing of personality, mind, body etc. Surely there is nothing controversial here.' The impression I gave was that I was positive but careful. This defused the potentially divisive situation in the parish and overnight renewal became respectable in Hawkwell.

Had I not taken a definite lead over renewal, I believe the church would have divided and the charismatics may have left. We ministers must give a lead. As one of my curates put it—sitting on the fence with both ears to the ground is a very uncomfortable position. It is also a recipe for chaos. It is asking for trouble simply to tolerate or ignore a charismatic group within a church. The clergy need to be involved carefully and sensitively, so giving a lead to the church. One does not have to be a convinced charismatic to do this.

Soon after my public statement about renewal the independent group which had taken over our charismatic housegroup decided to set up on their own elsewhere. I saw this as an answer to prayer. Furthermore, at the Annual Church Meeting in April, the churchwarden, who was seen as 'anti-charismatic', nominated the host of the charismatic housegroup as his deputy warden. At the same meeting I had stressed the equality between the two churches. My love for St. Mary's was a strong motivation. For the first time in many years one of the new churchwardens was from St. Mary's. Reconciliation was happening—or so it seemed.

The following month I wrote an article to discourage anyone from leaving the church to join a local housechurch. It was entitled 'Is it wrong to remain a member of the Church of England?' I gave various reasons for staying within the established church. The article was another careful attempt at reconciliation within the parish.

In August we had a memorable evening of prayer concerning developments in St. Mary's half of the parish. We were keen to have some housegroups and a church choir there. Also we had felt that perhaps the work should centre more on the church hall which was situated beyond the railway in the housing estate itself. Unexpectedly, we felt after the prayer that the church should be the centre of the work, not the hall. We also decided to move the monthly Family Service, which had been held in the hall, back into St. Mary's. All of this seemed to boost St. Mary's and aid the cause of reconciliation.

But my strong attachment to St. Mary's and great desire to see people reconciled to each other were not the only ways in which my human sentiment and sympathy were revealed. I had to learn the hard way not to counsel people out of human sympathy. During my first two years in Hawkwell I spent hundreds of hours counselling a few people who did not really want to be free of their problems. In fact, they quite enjoyed the attention they were getting. Some of them were just not prepared to obey the Lord and one of them was actually making up quite a few problems. To my knowledge none of them is sorted out to this day, and in each case eventually relationships became strained.

I had to learn that one of Satan's favourite methods with ministers is to get us to waste our time doing what seems right as opposed to what God really wants us to do. I think Satan is fairly satisfied if we are doing 'good deeds'—counselling those who don't want to obey God; visiting people to keep them happy; doing jobs other people should do—so long as we are not following the Lord's priorities for us.

Because of unhappy experiences with Parochial Church Councils as a curate, I realised how important it was for the church council to be a truly Christian body. By some strange reasoning Christians seem to have a double standard. In a housegroup they will try to be truly spiritual and Christian. In a business meeting they will often be fleshly and sub-Christian. I was determined that this would not be the case in our PCC.

In May 1975 our PCC discussions got very heated and various things were said which were quite wrong. As Chairman I was significantly at fault. So at the June meeting the first main item I put on the agenda was 'What went wrong at the previous meeting.' We discussed our behaviour and I took a lead in apologising because I hadn't chaired very well. Others apologised too. But for some this was the beginning of the end. They did not want such a Christian emphasis in the PCC and, therefore, at the next Annual Meeting, they did not stand for re-election. So began the long process towards a PCC who had all experienced renewal. How vital it is that such a key statutory body should be truly open to the Spirit if a church is really going to move into all God has for it.

Another significant factor about 1975 was the start of Saturday morning prayer breakfasts in our two church halls. The Lord really encouraged us in these and the prayer was quite deep. But sadly we only continued them for a few months until a new Sunday evening fellowship began. The latter, however, did not usually contain such effective intercession. No doubt this is why some of the developments in the church during our early years in Hawkwell proved ultimately to be superficial.

2: Disturbed by the Spirit

My evangelical pedigree was pretty sound. I was brought up and converted in a little independent chapel in Long Eaton, South East Derbyshire. During teenage I attended and was baptised in a Christian Brethren Assembly whilst, at the same time, managing to be assistant superintendent of a Methodist Sunday School. Then followed three years at London Bible College reading for a degree and two post-graduate years at Oak Hill Theological College (mainly drinking coffee!). In those early years, I was taught by some of the finest evangelical leaders and had plenty of opportunity to be involved in evangelism. I had seen some people commit their lives to Christ through both my public and private ministry. But I still felt my evangelistic preaching lacked a certain clarity and I found personal evangelism difficult.

It was in 1976 that my attention was drawn to what, in those days, was called Evangelism Explosion, or 'EE' as we later referred to it. They were offering courses of training in personal evangelism and I was longing to become more effective in this ministry. But it was American in origin. The title sounded dangerous—what sort of explosion did it mean? Their courses were called clinics, which seemed rather psychiatric. Would the content be high pressure, 'canned' sales technique? My sense of need overcame my prejudices and in March of that year I arrived at St. Columba's Church, Corby for a five day clinic.

The course was fairly intensive and provided a thorough grounding in the Gospel message. Basically it involved learning a brief outline which was little more than a set of mental 'pegs' which enabled one to remember how to present the Gospel clearly and logically. The outline was flexible. Another most helpful aspect was advice on how to introduce spiritual topics into general conversation—not something I had found easy. The on-the-job training was vital. One experienced 'trainer' took two less experienced trainees to visit the homes of non-church people. Over a number of visits to new people, the trainees were encouraged to take a greater lead until the trainer was taking very little part. We didn't find the team of three was too much for people to accept. One wonders though how the family in Corby would have reacted had they known that, on that dark night, they had been visited by not just one vicar but three—without dog collars!

I owe an immense amount to that training and returned to Hawkwell excited about the prospect of evangelism. My own personal evangelism was transformed and the time soon came when I began to train my own team. Initially, I took Patricia and my curate, Clive Sperring. At the first house we visited the couple were about to go out so we made another appointment. A week or so later this couple made a commitment to Christ. They have since moved from Hawkwell but the wife is still active in the church although her husband in recent years is not so involved. In the second visit on that first evening, I was able to present the Gospel to a lady. She was very near to a commitment and I believe she is still involved in the church, having again moved away from Hawkwell. Patricia and Clive were thrilled with the way our first evening had gone. Before that they had been a little sceptical.

Soon we were taking out many teams every Thursday

evening. By the end of 1976, 24 people had professed faith in Christ. But a strange thing also happened. It was just amazing how many problems erupted at about 6 pm on Thursdays. The rest of the week seemed relatively problem free, but not Thursday evening. Team members felt ill—just for a few hours, sometimes only until they were visiting the first home for the evening. Children became ill. Car problems developed. One member reversed into a passing car. Even someone as hesitant as me about demons and spiritual warfare eventually had to admit there was something more than coincidence here. I accepted such things in principle but often felt faintly cynical when people claimed they were actually happening to us.

We continued EE for a few years. With hindsight, it is clear that problems and weaknesses in team members' lives and relationships were revealed by the spiritual warfare in which we were involved. But we were rather 'green' in those matters in those days, and didn't battle in prayer as we would now. Besides, privately, I didn't want to believe in demonic opposition—except in theory. It rather scared me.

Meanwhile, things were developing in exciting ways in the church, and this undoubtedly increased the spiritual battle. In April 1976, we took over forty church members for a weekend houseparty at Mabledon, a large house in Tonbridge, Kent. I led the sessions on the work of the Holy Spirit and on the need for an open fellowship meeting within the parish. The Friday evening, Saturday morning and afternoon sessions went well, and seemed to have far-reaching implications for the church. We seemed unanimous in favour of major change and development.

Then on Saturday evening, we showed a film about the Church of the Redeemer, Houston—a large charismatic episcopal church. Unfortunately, I had forgotten what it was like—having seen it in a very different context years before. In itself, the film was good. In the context of the stage we had reached as a church it was awful. I sat there wanting to crawl under the floor boards, at the seemingly endless scenes of people in tears, people with eyes closed and arms raised, singing in tongues or listening to mumbled prophecies. I could feel the hackles rising everywhere around me.

To cap it all, an argument blew up after the evening drink. I wasn't present but apparently one leader had been playing worship songs on the piano and some people were singing. Other people were laughing and joking and eventually the pianist stormed off to bed, angry at the disruption caused by this hilarity.

I woke up at 6 am on the Sunday with a headache. I looked out of the window at the early morning sun shining on the gardens and felt utterly miserable. 'Lord, why have you allowed this to happen?' I prayed. 'It's a disaster—after things were going so well. Now there are divisions and quarrels. Lord, what are you doing?' Patricia did her wifely comforting to the best of her ability and eventually, we trudged wearily down to the 8 am prayer time. The atmosphere was like lead. After a quarter of an hour, one more sadistic member tried to cheer us all up with the most inappropriate song he could have chosen. 'This is the day that the Lord has made, we will rejoice and be glad in it.' Rejoice? I just wanted to go home.

Then it happened! The pianist who had been so upset the previous evening prayed a prayer of repentance and broke down in tears—very unusual in those days in the fellowship. Then one after another—men as well as women—broke down. I didn't, as I'm not easily moved to tears in such a context. But I knew it wasn't hysteria. There was a real softening of hard hearts; real repentance; and some reconciliation. It was covering a far wider area than the previous night's trauma.

After breakfast, we had planned an informal communion in the lounge. In fact, this lasted for some two and a half hours when the Holy Spirit continued to move in repentance, reconciliation and in other blessings as numerous people were prayed for. In spite of a Saturday evening that was an all but complete disaster, the Lord made Mabledon, April 1976, a major turning point for Hawkwell Church.

The following Sunday we began the Sunday Fellowship which met after the evening service at the Rectory. Its aim was to explore charismatic worship, ministry and fellowship. In spite of our experience in Cheltenham, we were still very 'green', but we learnt many things by our mistakes. It was, after all, a fairly tolerant and accepting fellowship. The regulars were the more charismatically inclined church members. But we encouraged everyone to come. For example, on Whit Sunday 1976, I wrote the following circular:

'Forgive this duplicated letter, but I feel a sense of urgency about this matter. I am sending this pastoral message to all leaders, and to those who have been involved in the Mabledon Houseparty and the Sunday Evening Fellowship . . .

'What I write is not critical but is out of a pastoral concern and a desire for obedience to God. I sense that God has been and is working remarkably in the lives of many. They have taken steps forward spiritually and I believe we are on the verge of a whole new phase in terms of fellowship, ministry and evangelism.

'But the devil is very active to try to stop this. He wants particularly to prevent us meeting together in fellowship, because fellowship will prove vital in God's plan for us . . . If God has been teaching us lessons, we must go on

*learning them or else we shall be worse off than ever. I
believe each of us should ask God whether it is right for
us to attend the Sunday evening fellowship. . . .*

*'I am, frankly, excited with what God is doing and
how he is leading us. And by His Spirit, I am determined
to go on in obedience to Him. This will mean sacrifice but
it will also mean tremendous blessing. Will you go on too?
. . .'*

One of the churchwardens wrote me a note in reply:

*'The main reason for my not attending the Sunday
Evening Fellowship is that I am not sure that it is God's
will that I should attend. I find the meetings tend to be
geared, as at Mabledon, towards the Charismatic movement (as it is normally narrowly defined). As such, there
is a lot that I find not at all helpful and, indeed, some
things that I feel difficult to pass over without immediate
comment. Thus, on such occasions I am not spiritually uplifted, at times the very opposite and have a sense of guilt
that I may also spoil the fellowship of others.*

*'There is no doubt that this renewal movement has been
of much spiritual benefit to some who in the past have
been the unstable members of our church. I pray that they
may continue to be blessed.*

*'There is a feeling persisting, however, that our goal
will be achieved when we are all won over to this form
of Christian expression, and I am by no means sure that
this is the way God wants us to move. The danger is that
if the few push the many too much towards the way they
think we should be moving, it will lead to sides being
taken: "them against us". I know from your efforts that
you are striving hard to avoid this, but not altogether, I
think, successfully.'*

Naturally, this letter stirred the old anxiety feelings in

me. But I meant what I had written. I was determined to go on in obedience to the Lord. Happily the church-warden concerned gradually moved to the point where he was able to be fully involved in the renewal which took place over the next few years. Much as he had initially disliked choruses, he made 'Spirit of the living God fall afresh on me' his regular prayer and God changed him remarkably.

In my circular letter I had asked anyone with difficulties to talk them over with me and I did have a profitable chat with the churchwarden mentioned above. Often in the church hurts and tensions are largely 'swept under the carpet.' This leads to an uneasy truce with occasional traumas. However, the cost of this superfi-ciality is that the church is ineffective in its work and witness. Back in 1976 I still really hadn't learnt this lesson and many things were swept under the carpet—for the time being.

During August of that year, through the generosity of a friend, Patricia and I spent a ten-day retreat with the Evangelical Sisters of Mary in Darmstadt, Germany. The sisters are evangelical Lutherans and so refreshingly different from the English evangelicalism I know so well. We were immediately impressed by their love and kind-ness and by their attention to detail. They met our coach from the airport with songs of welcome and blessing.

The sisters established their 'little land of Canaan' largely with their own hands, experiencing miracle after miracle under their founder Mother Basilea Schlink. It is a mini version of the Holy Land with its own Sea of Galilee, Mount Tabor, Mount of Beatitudes, River Jordan and Garden of Jesus' Sufferings. This garden is a most beautiful, secluded area with very fine stone sculptures depicting the Passion of Christ. To be in the beauty of the place is in itself a deep experience.

The whole community lives by faith. They don't even

lay down charges for accommodation, meals or literature. The Lord has provided generously for the buildings, gardens and equipment. Nothing is shoddy; loving attention is paid to every detail. About 150 people from 18–20 nations and all denominations attended the retreat. At one point in the introductions comments by Japanese guests had to be translated into German and then into English.

The loving welcome, the beautiful surroundings and the stress on reconciliation between denominations and nationalities hardly prepared us for the shock we were to receive. On the Sunday afternoon, we were shown a series of sound slides based on the Book of Revelation. The slides were of various works of art—many of them mediaeval. Patricia and I were horrified. I rebelled as I never remember doing before as the truths about God as judge, punishment of sin, and ultimate condemnation to hell were portrayed. Even though the slides did not treat the details of the highly coloured imagery of the Book of Revelation as literal, still I didn't want to know. I wrote at the time, 'It was a strange, dark experience.'

When the slides ended, after a silence, someone started a worship song. Far from being able to sing, Patricia and I sat almost in a state of shock—just wanting to leave. Outside we began to convince ourselves that the sisters were as unbalanced, even heretics. We felt (quite unjustly) that they were gloating over the terrible judgements the slides had referred to. We simply didn't want to believe in a God like theirs. This wasn't the God we were used to—the God of Anglican evangelicalism or the charismatic movement. Had we not been in Germany, we would have come home immediately. We had always tried to be open-minded and tolerant at conferences. But this was too much.

There was only one thing for it. As good evangelicals we'd look at what the Bible had to say. In the next

27

twenty-four hours, I scan-read the New Testament marking the references to judgment, repentance, persecution and other similar subjects which seemed rather gloomy to me at the time. Slowly the realisation dawned on me that I wasn't such a good evangelical after all. In theory, I definitely accepted the teaching of Scripture. But emotionally I had partly rejected many of the passages on these difficult subjects. I found I didn't really want to believe in a Jesus who 'is revealed from heaven in blazing fire with his powerful angels', and 'will punish those who do not know God and do not obey the gospel of our Lord Jesus', and who warns that they 'will be punished with everlasting destruction and shut out from the presence of the Lord . . .'. Yet this passage was not in the highly symbolical Book of Revelation, but there in 2 Thessalonians! The more I read, the more I realised how much the New Testament teaches God's judgment; training through suffering and persecution; the importance of repentance and the reality of hell. But now, instead of rebelling, I allowed the Holy Spirit gently to bring me to terms with the pain and the threat of such things.

As never before, I began to appreciate the condemnation Jesus bore on the cross to save us. The sisters' Passion meditation helped us. It consisted of four 90-minute sessions of readings, prayers and songs and was a very moving and deep spiritual experience. But also I began to appreciate the reality of what the modern funeral service calls 'the pains of eternal death'. I saw much more clearly the urgent need to urge, even to warn people to respond in repentance and faith to God's rescue mission in Christ so that they may be saved from such an eternal destiny. On the other hand, I began to see how diabolical is the heresy that 'we all get to heaven in the end' or 'universalism' as it is called. I fear that if we are not careful we lull people into a false sense of eternal security when they have not responded to Christ. We must, of course, be sensitive in a funeral service, especially as we do not know what goes on in a person's heart, even in the final moments of life. But how terrible it is to give the impression that those who die in deliberate unbelief go to heaven. I believe universalism is ruled out by the New Testament. I couldn't bear to think that someone would experience 'the pains of eternal death' (as the funeral service puts it) because I had failed to warn them sensitively at an appropriate opportunity.

So our retreat with the Sisters of Mary, which included many sessions and events of a happier nature, proved a stimulating, challenging and disturbing meeting with God. We came home knowing the choice before us was to be either biblical or sentimental. Either we took seriously the New Testament teaching on the sternness as well as the kindness of God (Rom. 11:22) or we could go forward in superficiality. We knew that the latter would be unrealistic and desperately unloving to those who do not yet know Christ.

3: Yielding to the Spirit

Our evangelism began to raise some awkward questions which we had to wrestle with in 1976. Here we were, warmly inviting parishioners to come to church. Yet, frankly, I regarded the morning services in those days as rather dreary. A church member wrote to me in December 1975 saying, 'I am at a loss to understand why it is that during a service of praise and worship to God, there is very little joy and happiness evident. But wait until the end of the last "Amen" and the change is staggering!' He was right, the joy and happiness wasn't displayed until the worship was over. Our Sunday morning arrangements effectively prevented the whole family coming to worship together. At Emmanuel, because of lack of space, the teenagers and juniors met at 9.30 am and the infants met at 10.45 am—the same time as the service. The pattern at St. Mary's was similar and neither church had a crèche. Little wonder that only about 60 adults attended Emmanuel morning service (70 or 80 in the evening) and a small number of mainly elderly folk attended St. Mary's. The monthly Family Services at Emmanuel Church and St. Mary's Hall were the only bright spots when the buildings were full.

We also began to take seriously the fact that some people had never been to church in their lives. They did not know what happened in a service and some were clearly rather apprehensive about coming lest they made fools of themselves. We might be quite at home with the complicated procedure using prayer book, Bible and two hymn books, but they would be totally confused by it all. We Anglicans can be rather selfish and thoughtless about these problems which newcomers face. Apart from a childhood experience of a scout parade service the first Anglican Service I ever attended was Prayer Book Morning Prayer at All Souls, Langham Place in 1962. I hated it—trying to find all the items in the prayer book; chanting canticles and Psalms (why didn't they just sing a good hymn?). I was quite exhausted by the time we reached the sermon.

'What was the answer to these problems?' we asked ourselves. The answer certainly wasn't to dilute the content of the services so that they neither honoured God nor fed the regular attenders, but at least we could blend informality with the formal framework of the service. What is more, we had to try to see ourselves and the services through the eyes of a newcomer.

Spurred on by the challenging implications of our evangelism, the PCC acted and Family Worship began in May 1977. We changed the time of morning service in both churches to 10.30 am. At Emmanuel the teenagers met at 9.45 am in church and stayed on for at least the first half of the service. At 10.30 am the infants met in the church and the juniors in the hall until 11.00 am, when they changed places. So the infants were in church for the first half of the service and the juniors for the second half. At St. Mary's the teenagers joined in the morning service whilst the juniors met in the hall and the infants in a home. Both the hall and the home were about half a mile from the church.

A crèche was started in both churches—at St. Mary's it met in the porch which had been fitted with heaters. As soon as the congregation had gone into church, a carpet was put down and taken up again before it was time for the congregation to leave. That meant that even in wet weather the children had a warm dry area to play on.

So it was that we attempted to make it much easier for families to attend church together. We introduced children's items into the services and made extensive use of overhead projectors and other visual aids in both the service and the sermon. It was a major step in the right direction.

In stressing the importance of the family, I had made myself thoroughly unpopular in some circles by discouraging single sex adult groups. My concern was this. Women seem more ready to attend the church or its groups. They also seem quicker to commit themselves to Christ. The problem is that as a woman becomes more involved in the church, without her husband, he may feel excluded or even resentful of the time she spends in church. The members know her but not him. Both they and his wife may come to feel that he is against the church. Furthermore, many churches have groups for women; fewer have men's groups. So the old impression—church is for women and children—is reinforced in a man's mind. It is for these reasons that we discontinued the Young Wives' Group in favour of mixed housegroups. We also changed the Women's Fellowship—which had an older membership—into a group to which men could come as well. However, now that we have many mixed groups, I would not in principle be against including a single sex group in our programme.

Whenever we make contact with a married woman, we ensure that her husband is contacted as soon as possible. Similarly, when we contact children we also visit the parents as soon as possible. This way we try to win whole families to Christ.

My concern to see St. Mary's an equal partner with Emmanuel was just as strong as ever. To have proper

Family Worship we needed further accommodation at St. Mary's. In early 1977 I spent days of my time trying to sort something out. In the long term we toyed with the idea of a church extension and even had the architect draw up magnificent plans. One wet Saturday morning, we had our longest Standing Committee ever! One churchwarden drove us all over Essex and we stood looking at extensions to ancient churches.

The idea of a church extension didn't help for the immediate needs. Would it be possible to have a temporary building in the churchyard or even in an adjoining field? We went as far as to look at a large secondhand residential caravan. It even had a bath fitted in it which someone suggested would be useful for baptism by immersion! But the local planning office ruled all these out. The restrictions on temporary accommodation in the churchyard would have meant that even if planning permission were granted we would have had to provide a very expensive and attractive building.

Still I was striving to find an answer to the problem. So much so that when we used the tapes of the Sisters of Mary Passion Presentation in Holy Week, I couldn't concentrate on them. Nowadays I would recognise this striving as a clear sign of trying to do something either out of God's will or before his time. In 1977, however, I continued striving until the situation looked hopeless. Then the Lord took over.

In October, I noticed that the isolated house opposite the church was for sale. After a day or two it dawned on me that perhaps we should make enquiries about it. With the churchwardens' support, I contacted the estate agents. They explained that the house had been repossessed by the Building Society and they would accept the first buyer who managed to complete the necessary procedures. This would involve racing to complete a contract against other people who were interested. After further discussion with the churchwardens we ruled the house out. With all the planning permission and diocesan backing we required in addition to the normal procedures for housebuying, we would be foolish to consider entering a contracts race.

However, a PCC member strongly urged us to explore the matter further. So one Saturday afternoon a churchwarden and I looked over the place. It was dirty and dilapidated, but I remember looking through one of the upstairs windows at the churchyard opposite and hoping it might be possible to acquire the house. It was in an ideal position and the only house near the church.

The following Monday, the Standing Committee met and agreed to pursue the matter. On the Wednesday morning the archdeacon looked over the place and made necessary enquiries in the diocese. By the evening he had given us a qualified go-ahead. By 11 am the following morning, I had managed to book a surveyor for the next day, an appointment with the planning and highways officers and an immediate appointment with the solicitor. The Standing Committee met five times that week.

Although the house was made up of two cottages some 150–200 years old, the surveyor recommended it to us—assuming we replaced a floor and the roof. The building inspector made minimal demands. Planning permission was no problem. But the highways officers said the bend of the road was too dangerous for the house to become a public building. Again, I began to strive. I rang the farmer asking if we could buy or rent a strip of land for a long drive to the house. He was not willing to oblige.

So it was that somewhat apprehensively I met the planning officer and the two highways officers on site. 'No', they said, 'it's too dangerous. We couldn't possibly approve the plan.' A growing sense of desperation made me determined to do all I could to change their minds.

My first rather impractical idea was to suggest they partially straightened the bend by taking some ground from the churchyard. The only value of this idea was to stop them going back to the office immediately! Then a bright idea struck me. 'What if we were to reduce the height of the churchyard hedge so that motorists could see right round the bend?' I asked. Silence. 'We'd be prepared to keep it down if it meant we could have the house,' I promised. 'Well, I suppose it's a possibility,' came the reply, 'so long as the present drive is only used as an exit and you have a new entrance constructed.' I'd have promised just about anything by then. On agreeing that we would sign a legal agreement to keep the hedge down, the plans were approved.

By the following Tuesday we exchanged contracts, having got firm approval from local and county planners, the highways officers, the building inspector, the surveyor, the archdeacon, the bishop and the (emergency) PCC. We had also secured a loan from the bank and got the legal aspects sorted out. After all my pointless striving over the months, the Lord had sorted it all out in eight days. *unlike slave trade + 30 years war?*

Two weeks later we held our first full-scale Parish Weekend Houseparty at Herne Bay Court in Kent. Over 150 churchmembers attended and the speaker was Cyril Ashton, the vicar of St. Thomas, Lancaster, a college friend of mine. As well as greatly benefiting from the teaching on the Saturday, we also had fun celebrating Bonfire Night. On the Sunday morning the Holy Spirit began to stir us in a very deep way. Cyril was teaching on fellowship which he defined as 'not just meeting together but sharing deep down everything we have—love, possessions, homes . . . ourselves.' He went on from Acts 2:44–46 to speak of the need for a unity which comes from spending time getting to know each other and approachability. *+ Joshua 7:24 'rapidity'?*

35

But it was what he said on the point of vulnerability which struck me particularly hard. He spoke of the need to be open and honest with each other if we are to experience true Christian fellowship, especially amongst leaders. He continued:

'Some will . . . despise us. They will see our weaknesses and be critical and hurtful. But in no way does God give you permission to close up. In no way does He give you any permission to justify yourself. In no way does He give you any permission to resent that brother, that sister who hurts you. When Jesus was despised and rejected, when He was spat upon, when He was criticised, when He was resented, when people were hostile, when He was totally and completely alone, He bowed His head and remained silent . . . What right have you to close yourself to those who may hurt you when your Master . . . was totally and completely open. You will find this the most costly part of any renewal in the Spirit.'

As I listened to Cyril I realised that although we had been trying to enter into such a depth of fellowship, especially in the Sunday Fellowship, we were still only just beginning to see it. At the end of the session I apologised to the church members present for not having properly led them into that sort of fellowship. 'I need your prayers more than ever', I said. 'We've got to go forward. The text that's been in my heart and mind for at least twelve hours is . . . "Choose you this day whom you will serve." I believe that is what God is saying to us . . . He's certainly saying it to me. He's saying to me, "Are you prepared in your position to go forward into a fellowship such as we have had partly described to us this morning?" By the grace of God let us say together, "as for me and my house, we will serve the Lord." '

In the afternoon we had an informal Communion. The

worship was very uplifting and quite charismatic. Many of us had experienced this in the Sunday Fellowship back in the parish, but some hadn't. People worshipped God with arms raised. At other times people clapped and all but danced for joy. People received the laying on of hands and clearly many were deeply affected by the power of the Holy Spirit.

Sadly, this was too much for some people. Most of these managed to survive by sitting tight until the end of the service. But three couples had to go out. I felt for all these, especially after the teaching we had received in the morning. But I sensed that the afternoon worship was in the Spirit and that I could not, therefore, do anything to make things easier for them.

We were the last to leave Herne Bay late that afternoon. As I drove off in the darkness onto the motorway, my emotions were in turmoil. 'The weekend has been a success,' I thought to myself, 'but where do we go from here? It's fine for Cyril to describe such fellowship, but I'm the one in the hot seat. How do I go about it? Can I cope with it?' It sounds silly, but I found myself looking at cars we were overtaking, hoping one might be Cyril's. Then perhaps I wouldn't feel so alone in the responsibilities of leadership. I had no problems leading a traditional, even lively church. But what I was contemplating was different.

Back home that Sunday evening, Patricia and I sat in silence for a long time in the light of the fire. Eventually, I spoke. 'It's all a bit much, isn't it? I feel certain it is the way the Lord wants us to go. But can we really go that way? Can we really risk upsetting people like those couples this afternoon and even lose people from the Church? I think maybe a good number would go in the end. How does this square with the teaching on love and unity we have had this weekend?'

I sank back in silence, staring into the fire, reflecting

on the traumas we might face if we went that way. Deep down I think I knew I couldn't say 'no' to the Lord's call. But I had to begin to work through the fears of losing people and the hurtful prospect of upsetting people—some of them our loyal friends. Whilst the renewal was contained in individuals' lives or in the Sunday Fellowship, it would not 'rock the boat'. But as soon as it began to affect the structures of the church and its worship, there would be trouble.

The agonising of that Sunday evening was not an experience I would wish to repeat. By the end of it, and particularly the next day, Patricia and I had made a definite but rather apprehensive decision to obey God, being more adventurous in faith, in life and ministry in the Spirit, even though some people might be seriously upset by this. I realised that I had a prime responsibility to love and obey God. I was not loving people by disobeying God in order to keep them happy. God's will was the best for them as well as for me. So the most loving thing was for me to do God's will.

Ironically, the three couples who had walked out of the Communion all experienced a release of the Spirit within a few months. One moved away from Hawkwell and joined a Pentecostal Church!

Following our commitment to obey the Lord, come what may, we had to learn various important lessons. The first was in the area of finance.

4: Giving—a demanding Ministry

'I believe God is going to provide £1,000 tonight towards the crusade expenses,' said Don Double, the Evangelist of the Good News Crusade. A three week Crusade was planned for June 1978 in Hawkwell on the initiative of a local Free Church. We made Emmanuel Church available for a pre-Crusade Meeting on February 1st at which Don addressed a large congregation. 'So far, so good,' I thought to myself, 'I hope he's not disappointed.'

Then, horror of horrors, with me sitting in a prominent position next to him he continued, 'Who has the faith to believe for £1,000 tonight?' Some people put their hands up. My right arm flapped around at my side rather like a wet fish and I covered up my embarrassment with a benign grin. Thoughts rushed through my mind. 'They'll probably think I'm not putting my hand up because I'm on the platform. Besides I'm the rector—they'll assume I have endless faith for such things. Really, Don shouldn't put people on the spot like that. I need time to think about it. How can I have faith as quickly as that?'

By the time these thoughts had flitted through my mind the embarrassing situation was over and the collection was taken whilst we sang a hymn. The sidesmen counted the money in the vestry as the meeting continued. Just before it ended my churchwarden handed me a slip of paper. I announced to the congregation that £1,232.40 had been given that night. What a rebuke to my unbelief! Just in time to teach me a lesson for our own church.

In November 1977 we had completed the purchase of St. Mary's House, as we called the house opposite St. Mary's Church. We were also planning to buy a house next to Emmanuel (although this was later taken off the market). We had been quite convinced that it was right to acquire St. Mary's House as the unanimous PCC decision had shown. In January we began to feel we ought to raise some money to pay for it. First we arranged a day of prayer, then we called the PCC together.

I wrote in the March magazine that the PCC had unanimously decided to ask the congregation to provide £39,200 by Easter Day (March 26th). We planned Easter Day to be a Thanksgiving Day. Easter morning was beautifully sunny and the morning services went well. We had arranged for someone to travel between the two Churches during the service to discover the full total given. Before the service ended that morning I was able to announce that after four weeks giving the total was £39,280 in direct gifts and covenants. By the end of the month the amount was £41,663. The local and London press took up the story and the bishop wrote a letter expressing thanks to God and congratulating the PCC.

I have always had an aversion to sales of work, jumble sales and the like. I know people argue that they are an opportunity for fellowship. But the church should be providing fellowship in other, deeper ways. Besides sales tend to provide opportunities for arguments as well as fellowship. It is true that some people like to use their practical gifts to raise money for the church and I'm not against that. But when one considers all the effort put into a sale which will only raise a few hundred pounds, is it really a wise use of time especially if it is at the expense of the pastoral and evangelistic task of the Church? In ten years the sales of work in Hawkwell raised only £2,000. My main problem with sales of work is their image. Ought the church to be supporting the vital mission of God to the world by selling woollen tea-cosies or arranging jumble sales? It seems degrading to me. Besides I would not want to perpetuate the image of the church asking unbelievers for money to support the work of the church, one aspect of which is to make them believers! Sales of work and other fund raising should never replace sacrificial giving.

I did not close down the sales of work in Hawkwell, but I had no enthusiasm for them. Apart from attending on the day out of a sense of duty I had no involvement at all. In my teaching I stressed direct giving and the belief that God would provide, primarily through the local church, for any need we had if we prayed about it. By 1979 the annual sale of work had died a natural death. I was relieved to see it go.

From the early days in Hawkwell I stressed the biblical principle of giving. The October 1975 parish magazine was largely devoted to the subject. In it I reminded the members that all our money and possessions belong to God anyway. So he has the right to tell us what to do with them. He calls for the cheerful giving of a proportion of our income. Some Christians give sacrifically whereas others simply give God a tip. I pointed out the tradition in scripture of giving a tithe (tenth) of our income and then giving extra gifts in addition when necessary. This is not a law but surely we Christians want to give at least as much as the Old Testament people, who were nowhere near as spiritually privileged as we are. I went on to stress that the parish ought to be financially self supporting, not subsidised by the diocese. By that I meant the parish income ought to cover all our expenses including clergy salaries, even though the latter are paid by the diocese. Any 'profits' could be given away.

For years now it has been accepted in Hawkwell that giving a tenth of one's income is the norm. The same principle does, of course, apply to those with very limited means. It is the proportion that counts, not the actual sum. The 'widow's mite' is at least as acceptable as the more affluent person's tithe. It is important to stress that we have no very affluent people in the church. Most have modest to average incomes. About a third are not actually earning. They include married women whose husbands may or may not be involved, retired and unemployed folk, students etc. Many work in shops, offices or factories. We have a number of bank clerks, teachers, nurses and manual workers.

We see tithing as the basic minimum. Consequently we have Gift Days and other special appeals from time to time. The first Gift Day after our arrival in Hawkwell was in October 1975. We also advertised it as 'Decision Day' and urged three decisions on the congregation. Firstly to 'decide to give sacrificially to God's work inside and outside the parish (if that is not already the case).' Secondly to 'decide to make this parish financially self supporting, having money to advance the cause of Christ within the parish.' Thirdly for tax payers to decide to covenant their giving. That Gift Day raised £802 which was 27% up on 1974. A similar amount £820 was given in the October 1976 Gift Day. In 1977 we put a greater challenge to the church. We appealed for £2,500 which included £500 to provide sheets for a Rwandan Hospital; £1,000 for St. Mary's reorganisation and £1,000 towards a projected budget deficit. Over £2,214 was given which was adequate since we completed the year with a surplus. Two months after that Gift Day we bought St. Mary's House and later made the appeal for £39,200 in March 1978.

In 1979 we decided that we needed an Offset Litho printing machine to produce our parish literature and stationery in an attractive and inexpensive manner. We set a target for a Gift Day in October of £2,000 plus a commitment to higher regular giving. We planned to give 25% of the proceeds of the Gift Day to Missions. Just a week before the Gift Day a member approached me and offered to give £1,500 out of her savings for the Litho Machine. We therefore asked the congregation to give generously on the day so that we could give all the money to a missionary involved in translating the New Testament in Thailand. A further £1,500 was given on the Gift Day and sent to this missionary to finance the initial publication of the New Testament. But shortly afterwards a local firm gave us a quite expensive litho machine they were not using. So we still had £1,500 to spend. Eventually this was used to purchase comfortable chairs for Emmanuel. At about the same time an occasional attender at the church gave the money for a new organ at Emmanuel in memory of his wife. We felt with good reason that we had proved you just cannot out-give God! More bread less cash / diptheria

The Lord has honoured this approach to finances of prayer, tithing and extra giving. We teach it as a regular part of basic training for Christians. Occasionally we need to draw the attention of the church to a specific need. In August 1980 we mentioned to the church that we needed an extra £110 per week to meet the budget by the end of the year. By October the figure required was £220 extra per week. But we ended the year in surplus.

In September 1981, because of a large budget increase, we needed £8,391 by the end of the year. This meant a 114% increase in giving to £524 per week. By November the figure required was £762 per week. We ended the year with a £1,400 deficit out of £27,500 expenditure.

The 1982 income was £30,000 which included halving the deficit to £700. The 1983 expenditure was over £42,000 and we were £200 in surplus. Here are the main figures:

	1975	1976	1977	1978	1979	1980	1981	1982	1983
Income	7326	8366	10538	10378	16379	20561	26097	30161	42406
Total Expend	5960	7202	8534	8887	14775	17672	27540	30897	42205
Giving to Mission	496	846	1071	763	2702	3407	7110	9912	18883
Balance	1366	1164	2004	1491	1604	2889	(1443)*	(736)*	201

(*Deficit)

In the 1981 Budget the PCC decided to begin to give 30% of our income to Mission. It required a 60% increase of income over 1980 which was almost achieved. In the 1983 Budget after extensive prayer in the PCC we increased the giving to Mission to 40% of our income and also began a Care and Share Fund to help church members in genuine financial need. This Fund was a further 10% of our income. All of this required a massive increase in income over 1982. But the Lord provided and we ended the year with a £201 surplus.

Our attitude towards money in the Church of England can be seriously wrong. The diocesan synod had on its agenda a debate on 'The Charismatic Movement in the Church of England.' The clergyman who introduced the debate gave an excellent and inspiring speech, but the debate was very poor. It seemed as if few people had much to say. Maybe some were not very interested or informed on the subject. Following this debate there was a discussion on the Diocesan Budget. Immediately the synod sprang to life. No lack of enthusiasm now. Speaker after speaker launched into questioning and criticising the Budget.

How sad that the church is often characterised by worries and arguments about money. Frequently the church's task is curtailed by lack of money. I am convinced that the answer is the way of faith. The attitude of our PCC was summed up by one treasurer who said 'If it is right to do a thing, the money will be there.' I am sure he is right so long as there is prayer, teaching on tithing and giving, and concentration on the church's spiritual priorities including giving to mission. So many churches have proved it. Many more have not—yet. There will, of course, be exceptional situations of a pioneering nature which will require external financing. But generally speaking the sign of a healthy church is that it is able to provide for itself and to give generously. I fear that the church's attitude to money is all too often a very bad witness to the people outside the church.

We had to face a very important question concerning our expenditure. Bearing in mind the material and spiritual poverty of the world, how much should we spend on buildings and equipment? Clearly a church building should be neat, tidy and clean. But it is easy to fall into the idolatry of wasting money on our buildings. After praying about this we felt that the church buildings ought to reflect the average standard of living of the parishioners. This seemed an acceptable principle to follow over decorations and furnishings. Consequently we carpeted both of our church buildings and replaced the pews in Emmanuel with comfortable upholstered chairs. (Not a bad idea for services lasting two hours!)

Similarly I feel strongly that the Lord's work must not be done with shoddy materials. It is because of this that we have installed a good Public Address system with a 12-channel mixer which can adjust the sound from various microphones. This is useful in blending a variety of musical instruments and is a great asset in movement or drama. Similarly we bought a fast tape copier. This copies both sides of three 90-minute cassettes and rewinds in three minutes. It means, for example, that Christian Education staff missing the morning service, can take tapes of the sermon etc. home with them. It is also useful in meeting the increasing demand for teaching tapes by other churches. These are just two examples of how I believe the work of the King of Kings requires the best facilities. So often, in this country, we have low standards in these matters. We need prayerfully to aim high and believe God will provide.

One other experience serves to illustrate how God does provide. In 1980 Patricia and I decided that we would, over a period of months, invite the whole congregation, plus family members who didn't regularly attend church, to Sunday lunch. We provided a full roast dinner for the 240 people who were able to come over the 24 week period. In February we put a box at the back of church and made a single announcement about it. The whole venture cost £200 and we, of course, paid for our own family. In October we announced that we had made a profit of 50p. God does provide!

5: Discipline—a demanding Responsibility

The chancel of St. Mary's, one of the smallest churches in Essex, was overloaded with Victorian furniture. On one side a huge prayer desk, an electronic organ and the choir stall faced, over a narrow aisle, the remaining choir stalls. The Holy Table stood against the East Wall behind a fixed communion rail and the sanctuary was on a higher level than the chancel floor. A large lectern obstructed the chancel arch. This arrangement was inflexible and wasteful of space. A large stone font took up several seating spaces at the back of the church and the pulpit was far too high for the size of the building. Behind the Holy Table the reredos screen, which was not a great work of art, detracted from the appearance of the attractive, stained glass East Window. On each side of this window hung two wooden scrolls on which were the Ten Commandments.

With the backing of the Annual Meeting the PCC gained permission from the diocese for a major reorganisation of the church building. It involved removal of the prayer desk, communion rail, choir stalls, reredos, lectern, pulpit, font and the sanctuary step; carpeting the floor and replacing the Holy Table with a smaller table around which was a moveable rail. The services were to be led and the sermons preached from the Holy Table. Interestingly, hardly a voice of protest was raised at this radical idea and the work began using voluntary labour in May 1978 just as we were completing the renovation of St. Mary's House. The Archdeacon, of course, kept a close eye on us as we worked.

One thing we had forgotten came to light in a casual conversation during the work on the church. We had not specifically included the Ten Commandment Scrolls in the application to remove so many items from St. Mary's. I think we had vaguely assumed they would go along with the Reredos. Unexpectedly the prospect of the Scrolls not being re-hung after the renovations proved to be controversial. Some people wanted them put back so we consulted the Archdeacon. He said he felt it was a minor point and that he'd be quite happy for us to remove them. That did it! Angry, even vitriolic opposition was aroused.

I was quite prepared to accept that we had made a mistake, but the Archdeacon had said we could remove the Scrolls and that was good enough for the church-wardens and me. In the end the opposition was so strong that the Archdeacon, reluctantly, had to 'go by the book' and tell us to re-hang them. I didn't regard that as a major tragedy, although the Scrolls did rather spoil the new appearance of the church. What did disturb me was the bitter opposition which was expressed by some people, even leaders, against the churchwardens and myself. I was accused of treating the congregation with total contempt, lying to the PCC and of being so arrogant that I thought I was the fourth person of the Trinity. Such behaviour is, of course, forgivable and I hold no resentment to those responsible, but sadly it was never put right.

One day I was walking along the unmade stretch of the lane on which we live, having a time of prayer. I sensed the Lord speaking into my mind words I did not want to hear. 'You preach against sin from the pulpit and the people agree with you. But are you prepared to come down from the safety of the pulpit and urge my people to repent individually and face to face?'

'But, Lord, that scares me to death. I hate a clash and I hate hurting people. I could never rebuke people face to face. You know me, I'd always back off.'

The Lord, however, was not to be put off so easily. My mind began to race over recent events. Yes, I was scared of people. I thought I was concerned about hurting people by speaking critically to them. But as I walked that day I realised my concern was not quite so altruistic. It wasn't other people I was concerned about so much as myself. I was afraid they would hurt me and reject me if I criticised them to their face. At this realisation my defences began to crumble. I saw how selfish I was being. Also I had recently happened to read Matthew 18. Verses 15–18 struck me:

'If your brother sins against you, go and show him his fault, just between the two of you. If he listens to you, you have won your brother over. But if he will not listen, take one or two others along, so that every matter may be established by the testimony of two or three witnesses. If he refuses to listen to them, tell it to the church; and if he refuses to listen even to the church, treat him as you would a pagan or a tax collector.'

I couldn't get away from this teaching. Jesus had said very little about the church which is recorded for us. But what He did stress was the need to approach a sinner directly to correct or even to discipline him.

The continuing bitter reaction of some people to the mistake we had now corrected in the church was seriously wrong, and it was dividing the church. How ironical—it wasn't renewal dividing the church, it was two wooden scrolls. All my careful, sentimental attempts at reconciliation were being blown apart. The reconciliation was superficial and the division was there under the surface, ready to erupt. Now it was doing so.

How was I going to react? Was I going to follow my own fears and the easy going spirit of the modern church and allow the whole thing to blow over until it was superficially forgotten? Or was I going to obey the teaching of Christ as sensitively as possible? Deep down I knew the answer but, again, I had to come to terms with the emotional cost of it. By the time I reached home I had promised the Lord that with His help I would obey him.

Shortly afterwards I arranged to see one of the people who had expressed his opposition in such wrong terms. In spite of my anxious feelings of anticipation, the conversation was quite calm and charitable. I asked him to repent but he was non-committal. We parted with a warm handshake. But, sadly, things were just as bad afterwards.

Matters seemed to be getting out of hand 'with a number of people reacting wrongly. The bishop was due to dedicate the church alterations and St. Mary's House in the middle of June at a service of Thanksgiving. I had a strong feeling that our thanksgiving would be hypocritical with all the bitterness around. So I wrote a pastoral letter to all the St. Mary's congregation asking everyone to put their attitudes right, as necessary, before coming to the service. But still the sinful attitudes persisted inspite of personal approaches.

Eventually, I had to consider the second stage of Jesus' teaching in Matthew 18. I offered to meet the people who had wrong attitudes together with the church-wardens, who might succeed in reconciliation where I had failed. But this was refused. The year dragged on. Nothing else significant happened but the atmosphere was uneasy. Early in 1979 most of those who had retained the wrong attitudes decided to leave the church.

Sometime after this, rather belatedly, I found the courage to share with the congregation the need to pray for the people concerned and to urge them to repent, so obeying the next stage of what Jesus taught in Matthew 18.

From a personal point of view I was very sad to see these people leave. If only the wrong attitudes could have gone, not the people. But since the people consistently refused to repent, the Lord had to remove them along with their attitudes. It was vital that such attitudes should not remain in the church, otherwise it would be severely hindered in its work and witness.

Sadly, on a few other occasions over the years we have had to take similar action including with one or two charismatics who have become extreme. Normally the person in error repents immediately, often before being approached. That shows a right humility and readiness to obey the Lord. Sometimes, however, people stubbornly refuse to repent. We discovered the relevance of Jesus' teaching. If someone is privately disciplined and becomes disenchanted or leaves the church, damaging rumours often spread. It is essential, therefore that the church knows the main facts of the dispute. Also that way they may be able to bring the person to repentance where the leadership has failed.

But we also found out the relevance of the final step in Jesus' teaching. I do not believe Jesus means we should ignore or show antagonism to the person concerned. Rather I believe He means we are not to be involved with them until they repent, unless there is some emergency or special need. Although this is the teaching of Jesus I found it 'went against the grain'. It was bad enough making these matters public without 'treating the person as you would a pagan'. This was against the spirit of the age and of the church. Besides one couldn't excommunicate someone without the

51

bishop's sanction and this seemed almost like a step along the road to excommunication.

On one or two occasions, however, we found that a disaffected person became so negative and bitter that anyone who had extensive contact with them was dragged down too. Their minds were being poisoned toward the church. So we saw the importance of obeying Jesus' command not to be deeply involved with these people out of misguided sentiment.

Needless to say, Jesus' commands in Matthew 18 must always be followed prayerfully and with a real love for the person in error. No hasty actions should be taken and only serious matters, for example, those clearly harming the church, should be taken up. I have found this the most painful area into which God has led us. It has involved me in countless hours of self-examination and prayer. I have had to weigh up the criticisms of those with whom we have had to deal. But I am convinced that we would never have been able to enter into the exciting stage in which the church and its ministry is at present, had we not grasped those nettles. Happily on two occasions, after a few years, there has been a reconciliation with those who had been estranged from the church.

We have learnt many lessons through this area of ministry beginning with the dispute over St. Mary's Ten Commandment Scrolls. We have seen on that and other occasions, an idolatry of buildings which is one of our sins in the Church of England, especially with our beautiful historic buildings. The building can become an idol whenever attachment to it stands in the way of obedience to God—when too much money is spent on it or when alterations to it which would serve the church's mission are resisted.

We also saw how easily churches are divided. In our case it was through two pieces of wood. I know another case where it was the position of a flower vase. Of course these things don't really cause division, they simply precipitate a tendency to divide which is already present. Similarly I believe that often renewal doesn't cause division, rather it reveals it. It is significant that of those who have left our church only four have left over charismatic renewal. The main reason has been refusal to correct wrong attitudes to God and others. *til next schism*

It is clear to us that the lack of discipline in the Church of England as a whole is a scandal. Leaders in the church are allowed to deny the creeds or biblical theology. Some even proclaim 'Christian Atheism'. Others justify sex outside of marriage or homosexual practice yet they are not disciplined. So the church and the nation are confused and offended. The church is brought into disrepute and comes under God's judgement for its cowardly disobedience. Little wonder that many Anglicans have felt they had to leave the Church of England for conscience sake. *How abt Judges 21:14?*

When I was at College, a favourite passage for my early sermons was 1 Corinthians 13:4–7. I preached on it challengingly time after time. With hindsight I can see that part of my motive was self protection. I wanted people to be nice to me. I didn't want disputes and upsets in the church because I would find them unpleasant.

But in more recent years I have come to see that there are two sides to the Love of God as revealed in Christ. There is sternness as well as kindness. I'd seen that partly in our experience with the Mary Sisters but that mainly referred to the End of the Age. More recently I began to see that to call the Lord 'Gentle Jesus, meek and mild', as the childrens' hymn did, might suit modern opinions but was actually very misleading. Of course Jesus showed immense kindness and gentleness. But He also showed severity and sternness. Yet He always acted perfectly in love.

53

A few years ago I listed all the occasions in the Gospels when Jesus acted sternly. They were all incidents I had known since childhood but this time I was taking them seriously. Before that I had never sought to experience these incidents through my imagination. I saw Jesus angrily rebuking the hypocritical Pharisees as a 'Brood of vipers', 'Sons of Hell', 'Whitewashed tombs' and 'Blind fools'. This didn't fit the gentle mannered Jesus I had previously imagined. In fact I had regarded His driving out the moneychangers and overturning their tables with just a trace of embarrassment.

Then I read again his call for commitment. It seemed that when a large crowd gathered around him, he was likely to say something that would upset them. He demanded 'hating' father and mother and renouncing all one had in order to be his disciple. Little wonder that 'from this time many of his disciples turned back and no longer followed him' (John 6:66). Many modern ministers regard the losing of churchmembers as something to be avoided at all costs. Jesus on that occasion lost nearly all of His 'congregation' because of the unpopularity of His message. I began to see that although unity is a very high priority, obedience to the truth is higher.

But there was more. Jesus was quite hard in training His disciples. For example He rebuked any unbelief in them quite strongly. After Peter had taken the courageous step of faith to walk on the water, then began to sink, Jesus didn't say, 'Never mind, you did very well to get so far, after all, you're called to be faithful not successful.' No! He said, 'Oh man of little faith, why did you doubt?' (Matthew 14:31). There are other examples of such a 'hard' approach by Jesus in the Gospels.

I could not help but contrast this approach of Jesus with the attitude prevalent in many areas of the Church of England. So often, it seems, we are expected to be

nice to people when we should speak against sin and
hypocrisy. In our concern to be the church of the people;
the church which always shows an accepting face, we
sometimes make little or no demand for commitment,
apart, perhaps, from when it comes to the collection.
This is a sentimental, humanistic, but unchristlike attitude; and I don't believe it works. Infant Baptism is a
case in point. *nicer than Hosea 9:4*

'No thank you, we're not interested,' said the man at
the door. It was a dark evening in 1976 and with my
churchwardens, I was doing some evangelistic visiting.
I don't think the man recognised me. Some months
earlier he had rung me to arrange his child's christening.
He'd been very polite and ready to promise anything.
I'd taken the usual line with him—explaining the
commitment involved for parents in Baptism, and then
leaving the final decision up to them. They chose to have
a Baptism and I obliged, wondering just how sincere they
were. On this dark evening, months after the Baptism his
real attitude was revealed, even though we'd said we
were from St. Mary's.

Another team found a similar response from another
family whose child we had baptised. 'No thank you,
we'll call you if we need you,' was the response. These
were just two of many unhelpful experiences with
Baptism which included the bad behaviour of parents
and relatives at Baptism Services causing offence to the
congregation. Interestingly it was the lay people who
took the initiative in the PCC to discuss a firmer Baptism
policy.

Ever since my college days I'd heard arguments for
an easy-going attitude to Baptism. 'If you refuse Baptism
the family will react against the church and the gospel'.
'If you limit Baptism to church attenders' children what
about the fact that some church attenders are
hypocritical?' 'We are the national church, not a sect, so

55

we should accept anyone.' I wonder how many proponents of these views are, like I have been, simply afraid of the emotional cost of taking a firm line and becoming unpopular?

It is quite clear that statistics do not back up arguments in favour of a liberal attitude on Baptism. Out of approximately 27 million who have been baptised in the Church of England only 9 million are confirmed; only 1.2 million attend church and 0.7 million attend Communion with any regularity. Such are the rewards of allowing thousands of unbelieving parents to profess publicly that they turn to Christ, repent of their sins and renounce evil.

One fact, however, troubled me even more. In spite of all I might say, many parents who did not attend church would believe that the actual sprinkling of water made their child a Christian. I could not have on my conscience this serious error. It is a terrible thing to give people a false sense of eternal security through a wrong use of Baptism. Ironically, I believe what many parents want is not Baptism with its commitment and involvement in the church. Actually they want a prayer of blessing on their child.

After lengthy consideration the PCC unanimously agreed that we should encourage parents requesting Baptism who did not attend church to have the service of Thanksgiving for a child instead. We have found that an increasing number have done so, although some who definitely wanted Baptism have in the end found another clergyman who was willing to oblige. I personally have discovered that many parents understand our dilemma.

More recently, the majority of the clergy in the deanery have established the practice of asking all couples who request infant Baptism to have a Thanksgiving Service first. This applies to church attenders too. Then those willing to be involved in practice in the church may, if they wish, proceed to Baptism. That way we seek to avoid giving parents the impression that we are rejecting them or their child and we hope those who really do not want to be churchmembers will be satisfied with the Thanksgiving Service.

Let Linda, one of the parents who requested Baptism for her child in 1980 tell of her and her husband, Kelvin's, reaction:

'When our daughter was born we thought that our lives were complete and that we had everything we wanted. However, since then, we have found out that there was something missing. Our daughter brought something very important to us that we never thought would happen—we grew to know Jesus.

'Kelvin was made to go to church from when he was 5 until he was 15 years old (when he could get out of it). At the beginning his elder brother took him, then Kel took his younger brother. His parents never went and he and his brother were the youngest in the church by about 50 years! Nobody ever explained what the service was about and, apart from knowing the service "off by heart", he was totally bored every Sunday.

'I have never been a churchgoer—my father was a Catholic and my mother C. of E., although neither went to church. My sisters and I were baptised as Catholics, although we were never taken, or even sent, to church. I did, however, find myself praying in times of need and I thought I was a Christian because I believed in God—but I didn't feel that I had to go to church to prove it!

'Anyway, when Laura was born we were soon being asked: "When's the Christening?" and we decided to contact the local Rector after Christmas 1980. By chance I went to the midnight communion that year. Some friends were going, so I went along with them to see what it was like. It was a very moving service, and I liked it!

57

'In the January, Kel got the Rector's phone number from the board outside St. Mary's and phoned him to organise a date for the Christening. He was soon aware that it wasn't as simple as that. It was suggested that someone come round and talk to us about it.

'We arranged a time and we had a visit a few days later. It was explained about the difference between the Baptism service and the Naming and Blessing service. We both wanted the Baptism service. Kelvin did not want Laura deprived of her "rights" and when regular church-going was mentioned he thought we could go along with that if it meant Laura could be baptised. Anyway, once she was "done" we could soon slip out of the habit.

'Once we started coming to church, though, there was no question of stopping—as we'd both found the missing link in our lives and we made a commitment to the Lord.'

Kelvin and Linda are now housegroup leaders in the church. Baptism can be made a divisive issue but I don't believe it need be. It saddens me that some Christians respond to the idea that Infant Baptism can be defended Biblically with incredulity or even cynicism. I was baptised as a believer by immersion so I have no personal axe to grind. I joined the Church of England whilst at theological College and had, therefore, to study Baptism extensively. I concluded from a detailed study of the whole Bible (not just the New Testament) that a sincere case can be made out for Infant Baptism if the child has at least one believing parent. If I didn't believe this I would have to discontinue baptising infants and probably therefore withdraw from the Church of England. I am also impressed with the fact that God is richly blessing many churches who practice Infant Baptism. If it were the serious error some people feel it is, I would find this fact difficult to understand.

Having said that, I deplore superstitious attitudes to

Infant Baptism. The child is not magically born again simply through the sprinkling of water. For all the sophisticated theological explanations, the wording of the Anglican Baptism service tends to give this impression to the average person. I know this isn't the teaching of the church but the language is unwise.

Ironically, having pleaded for more godly discipline in the Church of England, not least in some aspects of Infant Baptism, I could wish for more liberal attitudes in other aspects especially towards those who feel the need for believer's Baptism. Some of our churchmembers do not believe in infant baptism and have the Thanksgiving service for their children. So long as they have thought the issue through, I am quite happy about that. The two views of Baptism can and should co-exist in the church.

One problem arises however. Some people wish they had not been baptised as infants. 'My parents weren't believers, they didn't go to church, they just had me done one Sunday afternoon. I can't regard that as my baptism,' is typical of what many Christians feel. This is another problem arising from our indisciplined approach to Baptism. I can reason with such people that all the elements of genuine Baptism—coming to repentance, faith, the use of water in the Name of the Trinity—are present in their experience. But if that does not change their attitude, I have to sympathise. If after full discussion and prayer they feel they must seek believer's Baptism, who am I to stand in their way and force my views on them? To say they are unbiblical in being 're-baptised' rather misses the point. They cannot regard their infant baptism as a valid baptism. It is their conviction that they have not been baptised. The argument is about the validity of the sacrament, not about 're-baptism'. People can surely be forgiven for questioning the validity of an Infant Baptism in which the parents had not come to repentance and faith. I have not felt free to 're-baptise' anyone and, in fact, the issue has seldom arisen in Hawkwell. But the pastoral problem is real. If the Church of England does not adopt the right approach we shall harm people and even lose some of our most loyal members.

I am grieved at the inconsistency in the Church of England over discipline. A man who denies the historical nature of the Virgin Birth and bodily Resurrection of Christ is appointed Bishop. A clergyman who feels he cannot accept Infant Baptism, can in some dioceses be pressed by his bishop to resign. Several of my friends have experienced this and have resigned. Something is seriously wrong with a church which can be so inconsistent.

6: Worship—a demanding Offering

I refused to sing it. 'If you're saved and you know it, clap your hands.' The others seemed to enjoy it. Admittedly it is, I suppose, a children's chorus. But when children are not present and adults sing it I feel it is what some people have called 'a mindless ditty'. The occasion was an after church fellowship at St. Mark's Gillingham in February 1967 just twenty four hours before Patricia and I experienced renewal in the Holy Spirit.

I had always hated the more exuberant choruses and felt very inhibited about the bodily actions associated with them. In 1972, after we had re-entered renewal, I attended a Fountain Trust Meeting in Birmingham. During the worship I managed to extend my forearms horizontally in front of me, palms upwards. I found that radical action quite liberating. The following year Patricia and I attended the International Fountain Trust Conference in Nottingham. During the evening meeting simultaneously we actually raised our arms. To our surprise we found this helped us with the expression of worship.

When we introduced Series 3 Communion to Hawkwell in 1976 we also introduced The Peace. The book said it could be accompanied 'with a handclasp or similar action'. The result was electrifying. I had letters of complaint saying it was too much for people to cope with and it disrupted the Communion etc., etc. All we were doing was clasping hands in church. We persisted with the practice and fairly soon the 'similar action' took over from the 'handclasp'. Some people embraced one another and greeted one another informally. They were committing the cardinal sin of expressing affection and happiness in the middle of the Communion Service! The church survived all this but still the worship was often dreary. We had however glimpsed more spontaneous worship at the 1976 Mabledon houseparty and the Sunday Fellowship.

When, as a result of the evangelism, we began Family Worship in 1977 the PCC approved more informal worship with choruses, testimonies and the sharing in church of prayer topics. The Parish Herne Bay Houseparty in November again afforded us a brief experience of spontaneous, charismatic worship. Until now, though, this more charismatic worship had not affected the Sunday services. Much of it had been in the Sunday Fellowship at the rectory. However, November 1977, saw the first of several big celebrations in Emmanuel preparing for the Good News Crusade in 1978. Jean Darnall spoke at the first and Colin Urquhart at the second. The church was packed and I had to lead spontaneous worship. So the congregation began to experience joyful praise and uplifting worship actually in the church building. Slowly it began to dawn on us 'Why shouldn't we experience this sort of worship as part of our regular Sunday services?'.

The Sunday Fellowship had begun to lose a sense of direction. After praying about it we realised that we had kept it going too long. The Lord had been trying to tell us that He'd finished with it. He now wanted charismatic worship in church. So on various occasions in early summer 1978 we introduced some more spontaneous worship within the services.

I was still privately wrestling with the implications of

all this. How far should we go with spontaneous worship? What about upsetting people? What if many people left? Should any services be completely liturgical? These questions were going round in my mind on the morning of Thursday August 17th as I had a prayer time, walking along the unmade section of our lane. Suddenly I had the strong impression that God was saying something very important to me. He simply posed various questions. Can I ever (including in the services) say to God, 'You must only work in this way or that way—i.e. liturgically or spontaneously?'. Can I ever say to God, 'We're not going to allow some people to obey the first and great commandment to love you with all their heart and soul and mind and strength by worshipping you with bodily expression'? Can I ever say to God (unless forced to do so), 'Lord you can only lead us for an hour'? Can I ever say to God 'You're not allowed to manifest the Gifts of the Spirit in this service'? The issues were crystal clear in my mind. Either the Holy Spirit was going to be Lord in our services and lead us in any way He chose—liturgically or spontaneously—or He was not going to be Lord. I could do no other than promise Him that every service would be open to His Spirit. I knew full well that he was aware of my professional responsibilities and that He is a God of order, not chaos. So I was confident that he would not lead us into change for change's sake or other harmful ways.

Three weeks later I shared my convictions with the PCC. With hindsight I think the reactions of a few vocal members were not as negative as I thought at the time. But I'm sure there was a deep, negative resistance in the hearts of various members. The subject was made a main item for the agenda of the next meeting. It was then that I began to realise the seriousness of the situation. I knew God had spoken to me and I knew I could not disobey him. But now the issue was going to be the subject of a PCC debate and decision. The crunch had come!

I took our baby-sitter home and then drove the long way home through the dark streets in order to have time to think. I realised that, in effect, the forthcoming PCC vote amounted to a vote of confidence. I could not back down on this issue. The depth of God's challenge and the solemnity of my promise to him ruled that out. If the PCC voted against me I had two alternatives. Either I could ignore that, press on regardless and face the consequences or I would have to resign. That night the prospect of resigning seemed much more likely. But I knew I could not back off even if it did involve resignation. I had a month to wait for the verdict.

During that month we continued to develop spontaneity within the services. Some people spoke encouragingly about this, others were rather negative and depressing. It may be significant that four days before the next PCC meeting the first of our new weekly parish days of prayer took place.

On October 2nd 1978 we held the PCC debate on worship. In a letter and at the meeting I pointed out to the council that so often we discussed worship in terms of what the congregation liked and found helpful. Instead of that, I said, we should ask whether God liked the worship. Was it a worthy, wholehearted offering to God? Did it please Him? I reminded them that the Holy Spirit had in renewal brought various Old Testament features back into the church's worship—clapping, raising hands, joyful processions, dancing, exultant singing. Such things were biblical and seemed not to be limited to the culture of ancient Israel. On the technical side I pointed out that the Service Books allowed hymns (and therefore worship songs) at any stage in the service; various forms of prayer led by various people and a local tradition of bodily posture.

64

The debate continued for some two hours during which time everyone contributed and there were very few discordant notes. One of the churchwardens then proposed 'That the PCC agrees that our worship should be open to God as set out in the Rector's letter and gives him its full support in this matter.' This was carried with five abstentions. Three quarters of the PCC were positively in favour.

In March 1979 the Worship Committee met to consider various minor matters. Quite unexpectedly a major idea occurred to us and was recommended to the PCC. So far in the services we had been incorporating a (sometimes lengthy) spontaneous 'slot' in the services. But we needed to explore spontaneous worship more extensively. The new idea was to have a two-tier approach to Sunday evenings. At 6.00 pm we would have a liturgical service in St. Mary's, followed by a basically spontaneous service in Emmanuel at 7.30 pm. The PCC agreed that this should happen from September. (In 1981 the times were changed to 4.30 pm and 7.00 pm).

Now that the council had officially backed the development of spontaneous worship alongside the liturgy, another factor began to occupy my mind. Leading truly spontaneous worship isn't easy. Many people can make a reasonable success of leading a liturgical service or a traditional Free Church 'hymn sandwich' service. But spontaneous worship demands that the leader is intimately in touch with God; fully spiritually prepared in prayer and repentance; and open to the Spirit of Christ. The leader needs to be sensitive to the promptings of the Spirit and courageous in taking a lead which includes not allowing contributions to get out of hand. If the lead up to the PCC decision in favour of such worship had been daunting, the prospect of leading that worship was even more so.

During the Good News Crusade in June 1978 I had gone through a traumatic personal crisis. I simply had no confidence that God could use me in supernatural ministry. I was an adviser to the counsellors. People looked to me for help if there was a difficulty. I was alright when it came to leading folk in commitment to Christ. However, I tried to ensure I was not near any counsellor who might want to involve me in prayer for healing, deliverance or Renewal in the Spirit. For some years I had felt God could not use me in such ministries. I wanted to opt out of them, lest I harmed anyone through my lack of faith. I knew spontaneous worship would bring demands for such ministry. Similarly I had little confidence that I could 'hear' God and be really sensitive to him especially in a public context. All in all I felt dreadfully inadequate to lead spontaneous worship.

In June 1979 I was asked to lead a Holiday Bible Week at Haldon Court, Exmouth. This involved a brief morning session and an evening meeting. During the day I had a good deal of free time which I devoted to Bible Study and prayer. I sought to lead the evening meetings in spontaneous worship with some success. But of course many people wanted to receive counselling and prayer. Not having any of my leaders with me I was the only one who could provide this ministry. The responsibility of this gave me a tension headache at one stage in the week. On the final evening the Lord blessed the worship and the ministry of the Word. At the end I hesitantly invited anyone who wanted prayer to indicate. The response was overwhelming. There were simply too many for me to deal with through normal counselling. I was forced into the position of praying briefly for each one, trusting God to guide me as to their needs. I sensed God was giving me quite remarkable discernment as to how to pray and many people were greatly helped. This unexpected 'Baptism of Fire' built up my confidence

66

that God could actually use me. Little had I anticipated that my trip to Haldon Court was, in God's plan, a preparation for the new 7.30 pm spontaneous service.

Sunday September 9th 1979 saw the beginning of the new two-tier pattern for Sunday evenings. At 6 pm there was Evening Prayer at St. Mary's. Our intention was for this to be a straightforward liturgical service. I can truly appreciate such a service, especially in the setting of a lovely mediaeval church building. There is a sense of stillness and silence. The words of the liturgy can be quite moving. What could be more beautiful, for example, than the words, 'Lighten our darkness, we beseech Thee, O Lord, and by Thy great mercy, defend us from all the perils and dangers of this night.'? Such beauty has always deeply affected me. I can think of my Selection Conference for the Ministry at the Morley Retreat Centre, near Derby in 1964. At 7.30 am on a December morning we met in the church for Morning Prayer. The pink glow of the rising sun was shining through the East Window and the candles were flickering on the Holy Table. Then there was the quiet midday communion held around a mediaeval stone altar in a little chapel high in the gallery of Gloucester Cathedral. Just a handful of us shared in this solemn act with the strong sense of continuity with the past.

These are unforgettable experiences for me. But they also give me cause for concern. How much are they an experience of beauty and how much are they an experience of God? Can the love of beauty almost become idolatrous? I may come away from such a service which has been pleasing visually and aurally, feeling uplifted and satisfied, but have I really met God in any deep and extensive way? I know the one can be the vehicle for the other but has the experience simply stirred my emotions or has it changed my life for the better? Have I really offered a beautiful offering to God or have I actually

been indulging my own emotions and needs? These are
relevant questions to which I don't have the full answers.
All I know is that for me some of these services have
been far more experiences of beauty than they have been
living experiences of God.

The new 7.30 pm service was in a very different cate-
gory though. Emmanuel was quite full as I nervously
prepared myself in the vestry. It was for me a big step
of faith to be confronted with an Anglican congregation
for, perhaps, two hours with only four hymns and a
reading chosen (which may not be used) and a sermon
(which occasionally may not be given). I remember little
of those first few spontaneous services. They had their
good points but the emotional strain on me was tremendous. After the first half a dozen I felt increasingly
drained. One night I breathed a silent prayer during the
service. 'Lord, I can't take any more of these services.
They're just too much.' But the Lord gave me the
strength to continue over the months and eventually
relax. Maybe it would have been better to have prepared
more songs and items rather than to attempt to be almost
completely spontaneous. At least the experience taught
us a lot about faith (as well as a bit about panic!)

Initially we were so concerned to allow maximum
opportunity for contributions from the congregation that
we didn't give enough lead from the front. The services
were sometimes rather like Quaker meetings—waiting
for inspiration. On occasions frankly they were boring.
But always they were a learning situation. We have
experienced more and more adoration—being 'lost in
wonder, love and praise'. On one occasion, after such a
time of adoration, a prophecy was given which
mentioned kneeling before the Lord. Normally we
wouldn't have taken that as a literal command. But the
sense of God's presence was so awesome and over-
powering that the whole congregation (which was

68

standing) simultaneously knelt before Him. We knelt there in silent worship and confession for a long time. The experience was very moving but totally different from the beautiful services about which I expressed concern above. Here, in this spontaneous service, there was no doubt that it was a deep and life-changing experience of God. It was not induced by beautiful words, music or visual effects but by a sudden sense of the awesome presence of God. *vs Gen 3:22?*

On the other hand we often express our joy and thanksgiving in singing, clapping, dancing (just a little!) and sheer enjoyment before the Lord. So long as these actions are sincere, spontaneous and not pressed upon people they can be most helpful. The worship is often led by a small music group—organ, piano, electric piano, bass guitar, drums and sometimes flute and violin. The use of an overhead projector with copyright transparencies aids spontaneity in worship.

In the early days I was concerned at the lack of emphasis on intercession. But in recent years this has been corrected as the church has learnt to intercede. Sometimes a whole evening service is now set aside for such prayer. At other times the intercession arises spontaneously. One Easter evening we were anticipating a great time of worship and exuberance. But we sensed a strange restraint until, quite unexpectedly, we were led into a deep and sustained time of intercession for the persecuted church. It was only after this that the joy and worship developed.

We have experienced the various gifts of the Spirit in the worship. Many prophecies have been given. Some of them have been beautiful and, at times, moving messages of encouragement. At other times they have been expressions of the grief of the Lord over the world or national situation, or over the disobedience in the Christian church. The latter have led onto quite deep intercession. People have been healed on many occasions. For example someone had a 'word of knowledge' that a person present had kidney stones and God wanted to heal him. The young man referred to was prayed for and subsequent X-rays proved the stones had disappeared. Tongues and interpretation have only figured rarely in the services. More often, however, we enter into 'Singing in the Spirit'. This may be singing in tongues or in English with the Holy Spirit inspiring both words and music. It can be very beautiful and uplifting. We found it helpful to encourage people to sing words of praise in English if they did not speak in tongues. We also found it helpful to ask the musicians to stop as soon as they realised the congregation was about to sing in this way. Once the singing has begun the instrumentalists join in playing simple harmonies, not a known tune. There is, of course, nothing ecstatic or over-emotional about Singing in the Spirit. We remain as fully in control of ourselves as when we are singing a hymn.

The Lord had to teach me a very important lesson. Preaching has always been a main ministry of mine. I enjoy it and God has often used it to help people. Much as I came to value the Anglican liturgy I think a little of my Free Church attitude to the sermon remained. The sermon was the highlight of the service and the main item God would use. Now I still value the Ministry of the Word. It is not unusual to have sermons up to 40 minutes in length in Hawkwell. But I have learned a lesson.

Shortly before going to Haldon Court in June 1979 I had realised my unbalanced attitude towards the sermon and had 'given back' that ministry to the Lord. It had become too important. The Sunday after I returned, I entered the pulpit and began to preach on Isaiah 6 about the Holiness of God. I had only got a few minutes into the sermon when I sensed God saying to me, 'Stop, you're wasting your time'. I dismissed this thought but it returned even more strongly. I'd never experienced anything like this before so I faltered and then, to cover my uncertainty, asked the congregation to be in an attitude of prayer. After a few moments of hurried thought I said, 'I believe the Lord is telling me to discontinue this sermon and to offer prayer at the Communion rail.' So the surprised congregation sang a hymn while some twenty people came and knelt at the rail. The Lord did great things in the lives of these people—not through a sermon but through prayer. Inevitably someone afterwards told me she didn't feel she'd been to church because we hadn't had a sermon. But I had learnt a lesson. In effect the Lord was saying he didn't need my sermons in order to work in peoples' lives in the congregation during the service. On the other hand we regularly offer prayer at the communion rail after a sermon and many experience blessing. But on numerous occasions the Lord has brought people to faith in Christ, healed or otherwise blessed them simply through worship—before the Ministry of the Word. Each Sunday morning a different married couple lead us in some spontaneous worship before I take over with the rest of the service which is within the framework of the ASB. One morning this initial worship was so uplifting that when the couple handed over I continued with the same sort of worship. After about half an hour I asked whom God had touched in healing and other blessings. Several hands went up.

7: The Church Militant

I just didn't want to be involved. It suited me fine that my curate and an experienced counsellor from the congregation were dealing with the situation. A young professional woman we knew seemed to be having such weird experiences and to be in such a bad spiritual state that for the first time we were forced to think about demon possession. I had been brought up with a fear of such things. I'm not sure if it was this fear or just a natural rationalism which made me rather cynical about the subject. O yes, I believed there were demonic forces, especially in places like 'darkest Africa', or even in this country when people dabbled in the occult. But whenever I came directly across a supposed case, I tended to feel either that the person was making it up or that there was something wrong mentally. In spite of my reservations, however, in this situation, because my curate and the lady seeking to help felt exorcism was required, I discussed the case with the bishop who gave us permission to proceed.

I still didn't want to be involved personally. I had a genuine respect for the discernment and ministry of the two counsellors, but their ministry in this case proved ineffective. So I was glad when it was suggested that they take the young woman concerned to a retired Anglican clergyman we knew who, together with his wife, had been used in deliverance ministry. Off they went with my blessing, only to return disappointed. The young woman was still not free. Next we had a visit from Don

Double of the Good News Crusade who had a wide experience of deliverance. He ministered to her with only temporary effect.

I hadn't let on to anyone but for some time a worrying thought had been in my mind. I began to feel that God was simply not going to deliver this woman—even through these experienced men—until I got involved because He wanted to teach me more about these matters. I was very slow to act on this thought. One evening in September 1981 I went with the counsellor who had been helping to see the young woman concerned. She was in a dreadful state—looking sometimes like a frightened animal. By the end of the evening I couldn't avoid the issue. It was indeed a case for a full scale exorcism. And I had to do it. We made an appointment and returned another evening. After extensive preparations—prayers of repentance, and of protection—I began to rebuke the power controlling her. She seemed to be in agony and rolled around the floor. At times it looked as if she would attack us. I continued to rebuke the power in the Name of Christ with rather more confidence than I actually felt in my heart. I wasn't quite certain what to do next. Eventually the turmoil stopped and the young woman, though exhausted and feeling bruised inside, seemed calm. The Lord had delivered her and we were able to move on to follow up.

This is how the Lord took me by the scruff of the neck and made me get involved in the deeper side of spiritual warfare. I had previously been quite happily involved in the lesser sort of prayer for deliverance which I believe is often needed. I recall that the two year old daughter of a churchmember was very ill in hospital with pneumonia. I went to see her one Sunday afternoon and unexpectedly felt I should pray, not so much for healing, as for deliverance. I did so, being very careful in my language so as not to upset the child. By the Tuesday afternoon she was home and well. There have been many such experiences of 'minor' deliverances which have had clearly positive results.

Because we had been quite deeply involved in counselling people we had begun to see the importance of any occult activity in their lives. We had come across a check list of occult activities which we modified for our own use. Little by little, as we counselled more of our leaders, we saw the importance of this check list. So in 1980 we used the list with all our existing leaders divided into three groups. Each had a copy of the list and we moved through the various practices mentioned on it. We underlined any occult practices we had had any contact with. It was surprising how much involvement there had been—some of it forgotten or not taken seriously. If someone wanted specific prayer we obliged. But then, after a prayer of renunciation and repentance, we burnt the papers as a symbolic act of being set free.

After a time we started to use the check list with all new converts. We have found that without exception people have been involved and sometimes extensively. We don't make a great issue of the matter. Rather we regard it as part of repentance. We want to know that there is not even slight occult influence—which can cause spiritual bondage or fear—in a person's life.

It was in January 1980 that I happened to see a T.V. film on the History of Rock Music. It was fun to see the groups I had been interested in during my teenage years. But as I watched I recognised something I had not seen before. I could see not only an immoral side in some of the music but also a growing occult influence. It began to dawn on me what was happening to our young people. It is generally recognised that there is quite a widespread occult involvement on the part of some pop groups. This influences their songs and performances. I came to see that Satan was using at least some of the rock scene to bring the younger generation under occult influence.

One night some months later I fell asleep watching a documentary programme only to be woken up by the sound of a heavy metal rock group. I watched with great interest, particularly the antics of the audience. They were almost identical with the actions of members of a weird non-christian cult whose meditations had recently been portrayed on T.V.

So I began to take a greater interest in what had begun to happen in the second half of this century in connection with the occult or non-Christian cults. It was obvious that there had been a mushrooming of interest in the occult from horoscopes to witchcraft. I discovered that there were about a thousand new cults in the west, a hundred of them in this country. Most of them had started around the middle of the century. It was inevitable that as the Holy Spirit renewed the church, particularly from the 1960's onwards, there would be a satanic counter-attack of this nature. I realised, as never before, that we were involved in Spiritual Warfare. I had not wanted to face up to the demonic world. Now I simply could not ignore it. Even I was convinced!

The more I thought about it the less I could dissociate some of the moral changes of the sixties from this satanic strategy. There was the iniquitous 1967 Abortion Act. Granted that sometimes an abortion is justified, to save a mother's life. But hundreds of thousands of unborn babies have been needlessly slaughtered since the Act. In October we showed a series of Pro-life films in a local school. The wide publicity in the local press and radio brought good attendance. The whole event made quite an impact and was well worth the several hundred pounds it cost us. The film series was screened during a time of great national controversy over infanticide and euthanasia—topics we also dealt with. We recognised the demonic aspect in these destructive, even murderous practices.

I deplore the appalling attitude Christians have sometimes had to those battling with homosexual feelings. I would be the first to want to minister the love and power of Christ to such people. But, again in the Sixties, the legalisation of homosexual practice between consenting adults has opened a Pandora's Box of depravity and propaganda favouring homosexual practices. Even the church has been adversely affected by this influence.

The new 1967 Divorce laws again hastened the breakdown of marriage and family life. When there is an easy way out, couples do not make the effort required to overcome problems. Subsequent developments, such as permitting divorce after one year of marriage, are even worse. The Church of England is seeking to relax its rules against the remarriage of divorcees in church. But in the mind of the man in the street, it will, if it is not careful, be thought to be in favour of divorce.

All of this legislation brought about by the liberal humanist lobby largely caught the church napping. And it happened at a time when the occultists were saying we had entered a new Age from their point of view. I began to see the connection.

One morning after I had taken a junior school assembly an eight year old boy approached me. 'Mr. Higton, what do you think about ouija boards?', he asked. 'Why do you ask?' I replied. 'Because me and my friend are making one.' I began, in low key fashion, to warn him off doing this. It was hardly helpful that a teacher standing next to us said, 'The ouija board does work you know.' I did know, having dealt with numerous people who had dabbled with it. For example, I remembered the tough, nineteen year old builder's labourer who came to see me. He had been so scared at a party by weird happenings associated with dabbling in the occult that he hadn't slept for weeks.

Around that time there was a children's series on T.V. at 5.30 pm on Fridays entitled 'The Haunting of Cassie Palmer'. In vivid detail it portrayed a wide range of occult activities and included some quite harrowing scenes of a young girl calling up spirits late at night in a graveyard. It is true that we have found that new adult converts have often been quite deeply involved in the occult. But Satan seems to be aiming mainly at the young. It is hardly surprising. They are easy prey.

A Gallup Poll in 1951 found that 6% of Britons believed in astrology. A recent Gallup Poll, thirty years later, showed that the figure was now 80%. I think of these facts when I hear some Christian leaders speak in favour of 'folk religion'. Presumably they think that a little encouragement will cause this 'folk religion' to develop into full Christian Faith. I could not disagree more. Occult and astrological influence is very wide-spread and is totally contradictory to Christianity. Such 'folk religion' must be renounced not encouraged.

Following the example in the Book of Acts (chapter 19, verse 19) we encouraged people not only to renounce such beliefs and practices but to destroy all books and objects associated with them. So it was that on Palm Sunday 1982 for the first time we encouraged people to bring books and objects associated with the occult, astrology and pornography and to place them in a box at the back of church. At the end of the service we burnt them in the church grounds.

In the Church of England we are very conscious that we are the state church. After all, although most people in this country don't go to church, it is the Church of England they don't go to! We are anxious to serve our parishioners and to show an accepting face. We pride ourselves in not being a sect. We are the church of the

77

nation. In addition to the Anglican arrogance this might produce in us there are other grave pitfalls in this approach which we fall into if we are not careful.

One serious danger is of blurring the edges between the church and those who are not believers. Thank God that many people who are not yet believers attend services in church on a Sunday. They should be made welcome and introduced to Christ through the love of the congregation and the preaching of the Gospel. The danger is that if they have been baptised because of the lax discipline of the church they may well regard themselves as believers.

The Revised Catechism requires that baptised people renounce the devil, fight against evil and put their whole trust in Christ as Lord and Saviour. They are required to keep God's will and commandments and serve Him faithfully. If they show no real evidence of all this we are not justified in regarding them as born again. They are not yet members of the Body of Christ in practical reality. They have not fulfilled their Baptism. They still need to come to repentance and faith as the New Testament clearly teaches. If they never come to this personal response to Christ, their outward Baptism will not save them. They were baptised on the understanding that they had come or would come to that faith. We therefore do a very grave dis-service to people when we blur the distinction between believer and unbeliever or give them the impression they are spiritually alright when they are not. To me such practice is deeply unloving.

In New Testament times the church was clearly distinct from the world and remained so until the Emperor Constantine 'christianised' the Roman empire in 312 AD. Some church leaders do not seem to have realised that England is increasingly a post-Christian, pagan and superstitious nation which is repudiating both Christian beliefs and Christian morals. We are in a missionary situation. At least 87% of the population never go to church. By all means let us make use of the residual Christian attitudes and traditional attachment to the church. But how will we best win the nation? Certainly not by blessing British paganism.

I am convinced that we must first recognise that we are in a spiritual battle. The enemy is not simply wrong human attitudes but, as Paul stated, supernatural demonic forces. This requires a 'military' concept of the church, although this should not be isolated from other concepts of the church such as a family or body. In January 1978 I had written to the leaders about this. 'Now where did we get the idea that the church is a voluntary organisation?' I asked. 'Of course Christ doesn't force us to come to Himself. But once we have come to Him we accept His Lordship . . . The church is meant to be a disciplined body . . . an army under orders.'

In 1980 I expanded on this theme in teaching sessions on Sundays. I showed how the church is to be a deeply committed, loving, disciplined band of troops, not a conglomeration of isolated 'guerillas'. As a band of spiritual troops we must be committed and loyal to one another. We must be bound together in love.

The church, then, is an army fighting against evil and fighting to liberate those who are not yet believers. Such an army requires authoritative leadership, and this is, of course, a controversial area. But areas of controversy very often prove to be just those areas which the Holy Spirit wants to emphasise.

'It is generally known that you are exercising an authoritarian ministry,' wrote the incumbent of a parish some distance from Hawkwell. Quite how he knew this since he had never seen my ministry or discussed it with me, is another matter. Because often there is too little spiritual authority within the church, when someone tries to correct the balance, his attempt can seem unbalanced and authoritarian. Scare stories abound in the Christian church about an emphasis on submission by Christians to their leaders. We are led to believe that some are told when and whom to marry or how to dress. They have to submit details of all aspects of their lives for the elders' scrutiny, from their finances to their sexual activities. If they do not submit they are warned of dire consequences. These may include serious illness or even losing their salvation. Needless to say all this has little to do with Christianity. But then neither has the opposite extreme!

'I'm a bit of a rebel,' say some Christians with a proud smile.

'I am submitted to God, not man,' say others, (which is really another way of saying the same thing). Some churches have experienced renewal by the Holy Spirit, but they have been spoilt by the presence of many people who delight to 'do their own thing'. As we have entered into greater freedom in worship and ministry in Hawkwell we have had to be more authoritative in leadership. During the free worship there is always the possibility that someone may speak out of turn and spoil the service. The congregation will feel very insecure unless they are convinced that the service leaders will keep control of such a situation. I have never yet publicly had to rebuke someone or to ask them to be quiet. But on occasions I have had to speak to someone privately and to ask them not to make a public contribution to the services. If I had not taken this action the service would be ruined for everyone and more sensitive people would eventually stop coming.

The New Testament does expect Christians to be submitted to their leaders (Romans 13:1–7; 1 Thess. 5:12–13, Hebrews 13:17; 1 Timothy 5:17–18; 1 Cor.16:15–16). Without this submission there will not be that unity of purpose which is vital to a local church being effective in spiritual warfare. But we should not submit to anyone who is requiring something clearly unbiblical. Authority should be based upon a close, caring relationship between the person in authority and the person under authority. It should not be 'heavy' and dictatorial (1 Peter 5:1–5) but open to reason. Submission includes an intelligent expression of views and areas of disagreement which hopefully will normally lead to agreement. Submission is voluntary and cannot be forced. Only in serious cases of persistence in clearly unbiblical behaviour which is harming others should an authority insist on obedience.

The exercise of authority in the church should not result in Christians remaining dependent spiritual babies who can't decide or fend for themselves over personal matters without constantly running for advice. We encourage people to go back prayerfully to scripture and see for themselves the rightness of advice given. It is nevertheless good to ask for prayer and advice over major decisions. A correct use of authority should enable those under authority to be free to develop their gifts and ministries without fear of being suppressed.

In Hawkwell the issue of authority is only rarely evident, namely at times of crisis or serious difficulty. I would be deeply concerned if it were a constant issue. Something would be wrong. However in the early days of seeking to think the subject through and reach a balance on it there was inevitably and necessarily regular reference to it. Relationships between the elders and the membership are very relaxed. We have a lot of fun together. I do not stand on my dignity as the rector, nor do I exercise all my rights. Such thinking is alien to our concept of leadership.

A year or so ago a couple in the church wished to get married. They both had many serious problems in their lives including divorce before their conversion to Christ.

81

They asked for prayer and advice and we felt very definitely that in their circumstances they would be wise to delay the wedding until various difficulties had been sorted out. We reasoned with them but I realised we were wasting our breath. 'It's no use talking to you, is it?' I said with a smile, 'You've already made up your minds, haven't you?' 'Yes', they said 'to be honest we have'. They went ahead and got married in the Register Office. I was involved in praying for God's blessing on their marriage and we have been helping them since then. This illustrates that our attitude to authority is not 'heavy'.

We have set up various checks and balances in the church on this matter of authority. The eldership itself is a check that no single individual becomes a dictator. We make full and proper use of the PCC and there has never been any tension between the council and the elders. Two assistant leaders and an administrator meet regularly with the ten housegroup leaders and report back feelings, reactions, problems, questions etc. to the elders at regular intervals. The elders meet with all the leadership monthly for two-way communication. Most of the members are in weekly prayer cells and we ask them to report back what they feel God is saying to us as a church so we can weigh it up. Sometimes we have special times of prayer with part or the whole of the church when seeking God's guidance over a particular matter.

The system works and on occasions, after discussion, the elders' recommendations are not accepted. Recently the elders were recommending a particular house we already own as a new curate's house. The PCC felt this was not right for various reasons and we abandoned the idea. On one occasion the local radio station asked me to go on a phone-in programme on witchcraft with a panel of people, including a witch. Although a little apprehensive I was all for accepting the invitation. However I shared it with quite a number of my leaders. They prayed about it then conveyed to me that they didn't think it was right. I was disappointed but recognised that God was speaking through them so I did not do the programme. Personal disappointment is a small price to pay for the benefit of having leaders who recognise the reality of spiritual warfare and are willing to listen to God.

8: Structuring the Church Charismatically

What is Charismatic Renewal really all about? Some people seem to think it is only to do with a crisis experience of the Spirit which issues in a more intimate relationship with God and new spiritual life. But God has renewed the 'charismata' or spiritual gifts in the church as weapons for spiritual warfare. The gifts and ministries of the Spirit have a vital role as spiritual weapons in the battle to win the world. If the church is not structured charismatically I do not believe it will be truly effective in spiritual warfare.

In 1980 we realised that we had taught a good deal about the gifts of the Spirit, how the church needed to discover people's gifts and to enable them to use them. But it all seemed rather vague and impractical. We had no procedure for doing this. Yet we were supposed to be a charismatic church. After a good deal of prayerful thought we decided on a practical method. We would ask each leader to have a quiet day considering what he felt his gifts were. I produced a leaflet to help with this. It included a spiritual check-up and descriptions of the various gifts mentioned in the New Testament. The leader concerned would then meet up with his Leaders' Fellowship Group (we had three such groups with a total of 33 members). The group members would also have prayerfully considered what they believed his gifts were. At the meeting the group shared first and then the individual leader shared afterwards. This procedure worked well and the results were remarkable. After completing the discerning of leaders' gifts the housegroups took over to discern the gifts of the churchmembers in the same way.

We started the whole process in November 1980. All three leaders' groups began by considering what my gifts and ministries were. I spent a twenty-four hour retreat at Pilgrim's Hall, Brentwood during which the Lord spoke to me in great depth about my ministry and about the further development of the church. I felt that my main gift was in preaching—a more prophetic than teaching gift. I had been used in evangelism but did not regard myself as an evangelist. On returning to the parish I met with the three leaders' groups. They shared first and felt as I did, that my main ministry was prophetic preaching and teaching. But they also said that they did not regard me as primarily a pastor. Obviously I have done a great deal of pastoral work and still do. But I do not regard myself as particularly gifted in it, whereas I had seen other people in the church were gifted. I had to work hard at this ministry. They seemed to do it so effortlessly and fruitfully. The leaders went on to say that they did not believe I should be deeply involved in the ongoing, general pastoral work of the church. This should be delegated as much as possible to themselves and they would call me in when necessary. I found this so liberating. Here were 33 of my leaders taking the initiative to set me free as much as was right and possible from general visiting and pastoring, which others could and would do better than me, so that I could major on the ministries for which I was gifted.

But the leaders went further. They saw something which hadn't occurred to me, that alongside the local parochial ministry the Lord would enable me to minister on a much wider scale. I was both surprised and thrilled to hear this. It seemed so remote and theoretical back in those days. However, in the last year or so this wider ministry has begun to become a reality and is rapidly expanding.

One other very interesting thing happened in those leaders' groups as they discussed my ministry. Patricia and I had for some years been deeply involved in a prayer counselling ministry including to many of the leaders. We saw the Lord bring inner healing and deliverance from bondage, often in quite remarkable ways, in people's lives. But, apart from one leader who simply mentioned this, none of the leaders discerned that this was my ministry. Far from being hurt by this I recognised what God was saying. In the early stages of the development of a church, the Lord may give the ordained man various gifts temporarily, because there is no one else able to use them at that time. Then as the Body of Christ develops, the Lord largely or wholly removes those 'temporary' gifts because now others in the church should be manifesting them. We sensed God was saying that our counselling ministry within the parish should be delegated to others whom the Lord was raising up. In fact since then, apart from being called in by other counsellors occasionally, Patricia and I have only counselled Christian leaders from other churches. We sense an 'anointing' by the Spirit for those circumstances but not for the normal counselling within the parish.

We gradually worked through the whole leadership with this procedure of discerning gifts and ministries. Because we believe strongly in couples ministering together we dealt with each couple on the same occasion. They discerned Patricia as having a gift of prophecy and being used in intercession and evangelism (all of which she now combines in her leadership of the Outreach Department). All the results were recorded and we sought to ensure that people were functioning in the place in the Body of Christ for which God had gifted them. *unlike Torquemada?*

Not long after we had dealt with my ministry and the curate's we reached our lay readers. As we prayed privately about one of them I felt God was saying to me that preaching wasn't his main gift. Rather he was an administrator. 'But Lord', I reasoned 'how can I go to one of my lay readers and say "Your main ministry is not preaching?" I mean that's almost insulting. He could be very hurt by it.' But, as usual, the Lord wasn't going to change His mind just because I had difficulties with what He was saying.

So one afternoon, rather anxiously, I went round to see Duncan, the man in question. I chatted about irrelevancies for a while waiting for the best time to broach the subject. Then hesitantly I said, 'Duncan, I've been praying a great deal about your miistry. Because of what I believe the Lord is saying I couldn't leave it until the group meets. I needed to see you privately. The fact is that I believe He is saying that preaching is not your main ministry. Rather you are an administrator.' I stopped, awkwardly, and waited for some reaction.

'What a relief!' said Duncan, 'that's exactly what the Lord has been saying to me'. *He* was relieved! Not half as much as I was! Duncan became, and still is, an excellent churchwarden.

I had over the years been teaching and to some degree acting, on the subject of delegation which is essential to releasing gifts and ministries in the church. I believe in a full time authorised and authoritative ministry. I have seen untrained people in an independent church lead Communion very badly because they didn't know what they were doing. But I have never liked the clergy–laity distinction. The words themselves both refer to the whole people of God. 'Clergy' comes from the Greek 'Kleros' which means God's 'portion'. 'Laity' comes from the Greek 'Laos' which means God's 'people'. I believe that often the stress on a professional priestly caste has inhibited the development of the gifts and ministries of the whole Body of Christ. In the Institution and Induction service the 'laity' are asked if they will help the 'clergyman' do his job, caring for all the people in the parish. This turns the teaching of scripture on its head. The 'laity' are not here to help the vicar care for the parishioners. The vicar is here to help the 'laity' care for the parishioners. Ephesians 4:11–12 makes it quite clear that leading ministries in the church are put there by God to enable all the saints to do the work of ministry. The clergyman only pays lip-service to this teaching unless he delegates as much as possible. If he does not delegate, this is a recipe for inefficiency and will mean the whole church stands or falls on his activity. It can lead to a breakdown of the church or a breakdown of the clergyman.

I had written a controversial article in the August 1976 parish magazine. Its title was 'The Parish Pooh-Bah'. 'Pooh-Bah was a character in "The Mikado" who held many offices at once,' I wrote, 'and the clergyman traditionally has been such a person . . . In my 75 hour a week job in Hawkwell I've been preacher, teacher, pastor, evangelist, marriage counsellor, artist, musician, administrator, editor, youth leader, travel agent, taximan, delivery van driver, healer, children's work expert, child guidance expert, fund raiser, cheer leader, theologian, psychiatrist, gardener, architect, writer, diplomat, ombudsman, lawyer and a few other things! *And I shouldn't have been*!

'To be the parish Pooh-Bah may boost the parson's ego and calm his insecurities. But it holds back the church and frustrates the work of the Spirit. Gifts are not discovered. Responsibilities are not given. Training is neglected . . .

'No, I do not see myself as Pooh-Bah in the Hawkwell Mikado. Rather I see myself as the conductor of the orchestra. I am here to draw out and co-ordinate the gifts and ministries of the church. I am not here for you to help me do the work any more than the orchestra is there to help the conductor play all the instruments! I am here to help you do the work. And that's a full time job!

'. . . It is more important for me to train teachers than to teach; to train visitors than to visit; to train evangelists than to evangelise, although I would still teach, visit and evangelise.'

Needless to say this article stirred some reactions, not all of which were positive. One man said he agreed with what I'd written but I shouldn't have said it publicly. I disagreed. Such a change from traditional ministry would affect everyone and I wanted them all to understand the reasons.

Five years later in January 1981 we were ready to move into greater delegation than ever before. On the 6th of that month I had a quiet day to consider the names of various men who might become elders in the church. I had taught the principles of eldership in an open meeting of the PCC to which the whole church was invited. In this meeting I stressed that Paul had ordained elders in every church and that there was always more than one elder in the church. We had discussed the matter with the bishop and the PCC had decided to go ahead with the appointment of elders. On my quiet day I tabulated all the spiritual characteristics required in elders according to the New Testament. Then I literally awarded marks to the short list of names of men who might be suitable elders, according to how I felt they rated on the various spiritual qualifications. So I drew up my final short list in order of priority.

Later I circulated to the congregation a sheet which

summarised the spiritual qualifications of elders and also outlined the vision we have as a local church about individual spirituality, worship, fellowship, ministry and outreach. I asked the churchmembers to use this sheet prayerfully and to give me privately on paper their recommendation of men who possessed the spiritual qualifications and were clearly committed to the parish's vision. After receiving all the replies I was thrilled to discover that the church had recommended the same men in the same order of priority as I had previously put on my final short list. The names of three men were announced who would be elders alongside the curate and me. On April 15th 1981 I formally commissioned the elders.

We began to meet for at least an evening a week to pray about and discuss church matters. I fear that we sometimes discussed too much and didn't pray enough and those occasions were not so helpful. We also sometimes expressed our anxieties about problems in the church rather than turning them into topics for prayer. We had to learn these lessons the hard way. There was, however, by now, a great deal of prayer in other contexts in the church, much of which the elders were involved in.

One of our first major concerns in eldership was the setting up of various departments in the church. In my quiet days in November 1980 and January 1981 I prayerfully decided on the details of the departments which I would recommend to the PCC. They would achieve a maximum delegation of the ministry within the church. The present pattern is as follows:

A. Leading Ministries 1. Elders 2. General Parish Administration (PCC, Standing Committee, Publications Committee, Audio and Tape Ministry) 3.

Prayer Ministry 4. Creative Worship (Music, Art, Drama, Movement).
B. Housegroups Department (including Pastoral Care, Counselling and Social Events)
C. Young Church Department.
D. Outreach Department.

Alongside the elders each of these departments has a capable leader assisted by a team. The leader takes as many initiatives as possible and is responsible to the elders and PCC. The council approved a detailed, written Terms of Reference for the departments which facilitated their work and prevented many problems. The church-wardens deal with almost all the General Parish Administration. Linda Webb with assistants administers the Housegroups, Outreach and Young Church Departments. This means that Bob Wilkinson (who is an elder), the Curate and I are remarkably free of the details of administration.

We do not believe in change for change's sake but we definitely believe that church structures should be flexible. Not infrequently I will say to the congregation, 'Constant change is here to stay!' They know that in a sense I'm serious. New ruts are no better than old ruts. And, as someone said, the only difference between a rut and a grave is in the depth. For example, on occasions we have felt that our spontaneous worship service has got into an unhelpful rut and we have had to ensure it moved on. Also we have found it necessary to vary our methods of evangelism, our pattern of housegroups and our structure of leadership and communication within the church. The PCC has also adopted a flexible approach to financing our outreach, so that we can respond to demands as they arise.

We so easily find security in our traditions—whether they are ancient or modern—and become passionately attached to them. There is nothing wrong with tradition and structure in principle. Even the newest Christian groups soon form them. But God the Holy Spirit always intended the traditions and structures to be flexible. Our housechurch friends speak of old and new wineskins. The new wine of the Spirit, they say, cannot be contained in old wineskins. The word 'old' is misleading. The real problem with an old wineskin is not that it is old, but that it is inflexible. Consequently the new wine bursts it.

I believe this is one of the main reasons for the division of both the local and wider church down the ages. The original 'wineskins' (i.e. structures of the church) became inflexible. There was a new move of the Spirit. Instead of adjusting to this new 'wine' the old 'wineskin' resisted it. The inevitable result was a split. A new denomination was, perhaps reluctantly, formed. But in time this new 'wineskin' itself became hard and inflexible and a further split took place. I occasionally remind the congregation here of my concern. At present we are seeking to be a 'new wineskin' obeying the current move of the Spirit. But in twenty years time will we still be so flexible? Or will we have 'hardened off' as has happened so often in church history? How sad the Lord must be to see that he has often had to adopt plan B, that of division, in order to release his Spirit to meet the needs of a new generation. Division is always an evil, but sometimes it is the lesser of two evils, especially when seeking to avoid disunity involves disobedience to the Lord. If the historic denominations do not really and radically embrace the renewing work of the Spirit, the Lord will use other Christian groups—perhaps especially the housechurches (assuming they remain flexible).

The elders also pray about and plan worship, deal with serious pastoral situations, weigh prophetic and other contributions and relate to the wider church. We also felt strongly God wanted us to lead by example not least in the way we related in depth to one another. I believe there are three levels of unity. The first is superficial and polite. The second is the stage at which weaknesses and wrong attitudes surface which could easily cause a break-down of relationship. But when this is worked through, the third level of unity results, in which we accept one another and love one another 'warts and all'. We are secure enough to receive criticism and correction. This process was an important one for the eldership and much of it happened in the early months.

One major responsibility of the elders, though, is ministry to leaders. For a long time I had been impressed by Jesus' methods in this area. He had three years in which to set up his church and fulful his mission to the world. Yet he spent much time ministering to the Twelve and often to the Three (Peter, James, and John). The traditional Anglican approach is that the vicar should try to cover the whole parish in visiting etc. This busy, sometimes phrenetic, approach may appear right but I question whether it is God's will. Too often the church leaders are rather neglected because 'they should be able to look after themselves'. I have always believed that if the leaders are ministered to, they can minister to the congregation and the congregation can minister to the parish. That way, with the use of groups, it is spiritually and practically possible to minister to the parish for which we are responsible. So even before eldership we had Leaders' Fellowship Groups so that Patricia and I could minister to the needs of the leaders. The pattern has varied but we still regard this ministry as a priority.

By Autumn 1982 it became clear that one of the elders was not coping with the spiritual demands of eldership and so, after many private talks, I was faced with one of the most painful decisions I've ever had to make. I had to ask this man to discontinue as an elder. This was extremely difficult for both of us but the Lord brought healing and we remain in fellowship. Being without a curate at the time meant the eldership was considerably reduced numerically.

A worse shock was to come. In February 1983, quite unexpectedly, one of the other elders resigned. What had happened was that circumstantial pressures had come to a head in his life. When I saw these I knew it would have been wrong to have tried to persuade him to change his mind. However my remaining elder, Bob Wilkinson, and I were in a state of shock. We felt 'bereaved' and were in a dreadful state over the weekend.

On the Monday Bob and his wife Sue, Patricia and I left for an Intercessors for Britain Conference at Swanwick which we had booked some months previously. On the Tuesday afternoon we four prayerfully decided that we must seek the Lord individually and only share together after I personally, who had the main responsibility, felt I knew what God was saying about eldership. Bob had offered to resign if I felt it was right. We received nothing definite from the Lord on the Tuesday or Wednesday. On the Thursday we had no time for further prayer on the matter. I was beginning to wonder if we'd ever 'hear' the Lord on it.

On the Thursday evening we had a teaching session led by Bob Dunnett, an Anglican clergyman on the staff of Birmingham Bible Institute. The four of us sat at the back and listened to the talk which was on 'The Place of Eldership in the Church'. We had not known this was going to be the subject. In fact it didn't seem to fit in to the theme of the conference. Nor had we told anyone about the problem we were facing. In the talk Bob Dunnett said,

'If you've only got one man spiritually with you in eldership and six against you, start with the one. It doesn't matter that it is a small group but it does matter

94

that it is a group. Moses could not have done it on his own. You could keep going on your own for a time—Moses did. But you can't keep up perseverance on your own—Moses' hands grew weary. You'll never do it on your own if you want to get going through intercession. Moses had long times alone with God—but praying for the on-going work of the church is corporate. If you're in a situation with no one to pray with you, you're in the wrong place. Take your colleague off for a prolonged time of powerful praying.' . . . 'Don't be discouraged if there is only one person of like mind whom you can go back and pray with.'

At the end of the talk the four of us (who hadn't dared look at each other) didn't know whether to laugh or cry. So we laughed! The next morning one of the conference organisers said that she couldn't understand why the speaker had stressed this subject so much because it didn't seem entirely relevant to everyone!

So Bob Wilkinson has remained in eldership. He and I have entered that third level of unity where we accept and love one another 'warts and all'. And we can receive correction (or even rebuke) from one another secure in the knowledge of that love. Bob is now full time on the staff of the parish.

One of the characteristics I have learnt to be vital in Christian leadership and especially in eldership is trust. Without it relationships are undermined and will eventually break. Trust means being able to relax with someone, not having to mind ones p's and q's. It means trusting one another's motives even when we don't understand or agree with what is said and done. One question we ask of potential leaders is whether they have reached this level of trust in the elders and the rest of the leadership. There are those who find it very hard to trust or to develop in other areas of the Christian life because of hurts in the past. For this and many other reasons we have a counselling department in the church.

Some think the ministry of prayer counselling, involving inner healing and deliverance from bondage is unhealthy and introspective. It is true that there are dangers. As in any other ministry one does occasionally hear of bizarre stories of extremism. Of course it is also easy to put down all one's problems to childhood traumas. What some Christians need is not inner healing so much as repentance, obedience and a realisation of their riches in Christ as taught in scripture.

However we do regard this ministry as an essential part of our spiritual armoury. My own experience does, I believe, prove this point. My first encounter with this ministry was in December 1974, just before coming to Hawkwell. I realised I needed help and received a good deal from friends in the West Country. Similarly I found the ministry of those involved in the 'Wholeness through Christ' counselling schools helpful in 1980. I had benefitted greatly from these experiences, not least in the area of my private prayer life. But still there seemed to be something holding me back. I have made no secret of the anxieties I have suffered at various times in my ministry. Sometimes they seemed somewhat irrational e.g. being afraid of letters coming through the post.

During the summer of 1981 things seemed to be coming to a head. I had arranged to see two very experienced counsellors, one a clergyman and the other a minister's wife. But the meeting had to be postponed until the autumn. Intriguingly the lady had said she saw a very deep problem in me. In fact so deep that she was amazed that I had managed to cope with the demands and traumas of the fairly radical approach to ministry into which God had led me. I do not mention this out of any conceit, but rather to encourage others. There was a very deep emotional need in me which caused me great anxiety. But God was able to overcome it. And if he can overcome it in me I'm sure he can overcome weaknesses in any minister. But now, after all the years, the Lord had chosen to deal with this need directly.

The three of us duly met in November 1981 and I opened my heart to them as fully as I knew how. It became clear that there was a very deep insecurity in me which stemmed from my being separated from my mother (due to her being ill) in the first few weeks of my life. That trauma had been compounded with others like two months in an isolation hospital as a five year old etc. I really wanted to be free and healed of all this so that I could serve God better. But when, at length, my friends were ready to pray for me something quite strange happened. I suddenly felt a deep resistance in me to their prayers. Yet I felt this resistance was not really my attitude. I felt like a spectator watching something happen in me. The clergyman said he sensed the resistance and prayed authoritatively against it. After that came the beautiful prayers of healing.

The change over the years since then has been very deep and dramatic. The Lord has led me into steps of faith which, humanly speaking, I feel I could never have coped with without that healing. As I have said we have delegated this ministry within the parish to others. Space forbids details of the healings. But we have seen people mature as persons; become able to relate maturely to others and be able to serve God much more effectively. This ministry is a very important factor in enabling us to enter into spiritual warfare. We are not attempting to be amateur psychiatrists. Rather we listen to people's problems and through prayer and spiritual gifts seek to discern deeper causes. Then we pray for deliverance and healing including for the past as necessary.

We now have a whole department in the church which deals with prayer counselling. Not only have our own leaders and members benefitted from its ministry but also ministers, missionaries and other Christian leaders from elsewhere have experienced God's healing love through it too. It is organised by Daphne Upton who herself experienced deep inner healing. This is her story:

'All through my life I have been dogged by the hurts of rejection. A rejection which made me insecure, leading to not trusting people. Rejection by being unloved and so unable to show love. Seldom praised, which created an intellectual inferiority complex. Defensive, which formed a bad habit pattern of temper.

'When I was 3½ years old, my mother died—I cannot ever remember being sat on my mother's lap and being cuddled and loved. Upon my mother's death my father was a hurt lonely man seeking companionship in the Public House at nights, while I was left alone at home—a very frightened and lonely child. I sought comfort by sitting on the front doorstep watching people pass by. For this I was beaten.

'I lived away from home during the War. In 6 years I lived in 10 different homes—this made me a very insecure person. Many times I was made to feel second rate and an intruder and reduced to the status of a servant girl. I think of one home where I did feel secure and wanted, only to have the joy of achieving my 11+ exam taken away by the negative comment that it couldn't have been my maths that got me through—no praise, only the deep feeling of rejection and inferiority. I think of the teacher who constantly implied that because maths was my weak subject I was a failure in everything. Also there was the woman who used me as her servant and when I didn't meet her expectations, severely criticised me. From that moment I made a decision never ever to let anyone walk on me again—I built up a defence like a wall around me in the form of a temper.

'By this time my father had remarried. How glad I was, now I was like other children with a Mum and Dad—and so I returned home. This time I experienced a rejection which was far worse than any other. I arrived to find a whole new family—mother, father and a baby and no room for me. The rejection was worse because here was where I ought to have found love and there was none for me. So into teenage years, all the traumas of childhood pushed deeper down inside. I had learnt to put on masks, to pretend. It was like a pond, the surface reasonably quiet but beneath it was sludge fermenting, poisoning everything—so into adulthood.

'Early in 1980 I had to admit that I was not living the life God had given me in the freedom He intended. I went to Tony and Patricia to receive counselling for inner healing. They listened and brought me to the place where I could receive prayer for healing. I remember Patricia praying step by step through the areas of hurt. I remember at the same time hearing the Lord's voice saying He is not bound by time—my past, present and future are as one to Him—and so Jesus the Healer took my hand. He was there with me at my mother's death putting His loving arms around me, giving me all the love and understanding that a 3½ year old needed. He was with me in those nights when I was alone. It was as if He was putting out His Hand warding off the blows from the beatings I received. Jesus shared my joy of achievement in passing my exams. At the same time he showed me why this lady reacted as she did—there was a deep sadness in her heart. Jesus showed me I no longer need feel intellectually a failure, He made me as I am and that I was to use what He had given me.

'He has touched the memories of the past, no longer have they the power to hurt. The bottom of the pond is dredged, the water is fresh and clear. No longer am I

99

second rate, no longer need I feel rejected. I am valuable in the eyes of God—I am the daughter of the King.'

9: Vision for Outreach

'I knew one church that died from Koinonia'. I've always remembered this remark made to me by Harry Sutton, Canon Missioner of the South American Missionary Society back in 1976. 'Koinonia' is the Greek word for 'fellowship'. Harry meant that a church could die spiritually by concentrating too much on the depth and cosiness of its fellowship. I remember reacting against what he was saying at the time. After all, God was in those days stressing the importance of our building a strong fellowship here. This had been a major emphasis of our leaders' Houseparty in April 1976 at Mabledon which had led to the establishment of the Sunday Fellowship at the Rectory. I knew what Harry said was correct, but I felt that stressing it at that time could undermine the necessary emphasis on fellowship. And after all we were just about to start Evangelism Explosion visiting.

By 1980 the evangelism programme had rather lost its way and dwindled. The curate was leading a small but effective programme, apart from which evangelism was somewhat haphazard. I was deeply involved in the restructuring of the pattern of ministry, fellowship and worship in the church and had little time and energy to spend on evangelism. Then David Pawson spoke at a meeting in Southend in March. I was on the platform as part of the team who had organised the event. David gave a powerful and challenging talk on the urgent need for the church to be outward looking. He was critical of the inward-looking nature of many churches. Over the years I have normally been open to hear what people had to say even if I didn't agree with it. But that night I grew more and more angry inside. I knew it was possible to make all sorts of excuses for not evangelising. But a church needs to be ready for a major emphasis on outreach. It has to be fit to care for people and encourage them. It needs nurture groups, supportive fellowship, relevant worship and a high degree of unity. Whilst this is being achieved it may only be possible to do a little in the way of evangelism. The timing of David's talk seemed to be undermining this necessary emphasis in Hawkwell. I was surprised at the strength of my negative reaction—even for days after the meeting. (I should add that David has since become a personal friend!)

With hindsight I believe God was simply warning us not to become too inward looking and not to forget the aim of the renewal of the church. In January 1981 we spent a Sunday evening in prayer about the Evening Praise spontaneous worship service we held each week. Through various prophetic messages we sensed God was going to make us more outward looking on a Sunday evening. More than one person had a mental picture of a circle of people facing inwards then beginning to face outwards. We felt however that this would take sometime and we did not need to take immediate action.

It was not until September 1981 that we felt an urgent need to spend an evening of prayer about evangelism. The evening was well attended and people had prepared carefully for it. The three hours we spent together passed very quickly. What we sensed God was saying to us seemed exciting. He was going to do a new thing in evangelism—bigger than we expected. We must not rely on our past experience. This new evangelism would involve the use of the gifts of the Spirit like healing. Now was the time to evangelise—inexperienced and apprehensive as we may be. The task was urgent. We must reach out lovingly to people, providing 'halfway houses' between local society and the church. House-groups would be vital here so long as they were outward looking. The Lord also assured us that simultaneously he would deal with the church in a new way removing hurts, lack of love and disunity so that we could be used by him more effectively. Following this meeting we set various people free from other responsibilities in the church so that they could major on evangelism. During December we held four 'Faith Sharing' evenings in various homes. Neighbours were invited in for coffee, carols and chat with an evangelistic emphasis. These did not prove very successful.

By this time Evening Praise seemed to have lost a clear overall sense of direction. The leadership met to pray and we felt that the time was overdue for a new outward-looking emphasis. In January 1982 I wrote in the weekly newsletter that some evenings could be united with other churches; some could be spent in intercession or be turned into a teach-in on mission. Other Sunday evenings could be spent in evangelism, for example Guest Services.

We began to hold monthly evangelistic Guest Services, alternating between the morning and evening services in Emmanuel. 'There is no way we can bring people straight into the normal Evening Praise' I thought to myself. 'They'd never cope with the spontaneity, or the depth of worship. Probably the handclapping would put them off. And if anyone danced in the aisles that would be sure to upset visitors.'

So for the first evening Guest Service I planned a more structured service with hymns, readings and the like. I realised my mistake during the service, although, thank God, some people responded to the invitation to commit their lives to Christ. Since then we have not restrained the praise and worship. Time and time again we have found that the worship has deeply affected visitors. True they may have experienced a little 'culture shock' initially but the Lord has used this very positively. We seek to be sensitive to newcomers—explaining what is happening and ensuring they feel free to be themselves.

We always try to incorporate a personal testimony from someone as to how they came to faith in Christ. Almost always this has been used by the Holy Spirit very powerfully. So has movement and drama. One Good Friday morning the Movement Team did a portrayal of the Crucifixion and the removal of the Lord's body from the Cross. Suitable music was played but no words were spoken. The whole thing was so beautiful that there was hardly a dry eye in the church by the end. The message had been conveyed as eloquently as any preacher could have achieved.

The Drama Team has been similarly used. It is amazing how a humorous sketch can end with a very effective and solemn challenge. One such was the clown who preferred to live in a large dustbin, at first refusing to be coaxed out into the beautiful world outside. When eventually he came out he was overjoyed at the new world he had entered. This simple sketch with skilful dialogue spoke volumes to the congregation of new life with Christ. I have often found it very helpful to preach immediately after such a movement or drama, without even a song in between. They seem to open people's hearts and minds ready to receive the preached Word of God.

We have also discovered by experience the importance of Jesus' command to preach the Kingdom *and* heal the sick. Our evangelism often has seemed to be most effective when in the context of prayer for healing. We have experimented with various methods of inviting people to respond to the evangelistic challenge. As a result we have found it best to invite people to come and kneel at the

104

Communion Rail towards the end of the service if they need help. This may be to commit their lives to Christ; or to receive physical or emotional healing; or to experience Renewal in the Spirit or to find some other help. Every person is privately counselled, prayed for and followed up. But the congregation does not know why they have gone forward to the rail. So we challenge someone to make a public response but avoid exposing or embarrassing them.

At an evening Guest Service at Emmanuel in January 1981 there were a good number of visitors. Three people committed their lives to Christ and two received help because they were unsure of their standing before God. Various people received prayer for physical or emotional healing. One person who was quite deaf received a large measure of healing to the extent that when someone near her coughed, she jumped! Another person had back trouble and we discovered in her a not uncommon problem—one of her legs was about an inch shorter than the other. This naturally set up strain in her back. As she sat on an upright chair at the front of the church the difference was obvious and she could not correct it by changing her posture. We prayed and after a short time saw the short leg adjust to the same length as the other. Following some initial discomfort she was free from pain.

During 1982 we saw about 40 people commit their lives to Christ and enter a follow-up group. The Guest Services often proved to be a time of 'reaping' but in many cases the people who responded had previously received a good deal of private help from churchmembers.

There was, however, another area of outreach which had proved rather frustrating. This was the area of our concern for overseas mission. Ever since my college days it had been drummed into me that a church should have a missionary interest. Actually I had always been

105

interested myself. As a child I used to be thrilled with hearing missionary stories. True it was a romantic image. But at least it instilled in me some awareness of world needs and a determination to do something with my life to meet those needs. I'm afraid I could see myself as the missionary doctor, complete with pith helmet ministering to crowds of grinning natives under palm trees. I remember sharing an interest with my two young cousins, in a mission working in the Sahara. We decided we wanted to send them a gift so we wrote to them in Tamanrasset. They sent us a list of things they couldn't obtain and we sent them a box of Cornflakes. The man at the Post Office was filling in the Customs slip. 'What is in the parcel?' he asked me. 'Er . . . Cornflakes,' I stammered, feeling faintly embarrassed. I think he kept a straight face.

When Patricia and I were students at London Bible College we were both interested in becoming missionaries and we attended a house party in Holland organised by the Overseas Missionary Fellowship. Ironically it was during that holiday that we felt God was telling us to stay and minister in England. We were quite disappointed. A few months later I began to sense a call to the Ministry. From then on my concern for missionary matters waned somewhat.

When I arrived in Hawkwell the church was supporting five missionary societies with 10% of its weekly income. But the interest was really limited to a few enthusiasts—mostly women. We inherited an Annual Missionary Garden Party at the Rectory. Hardly being able to bear the prospect of such a potentially dreary occasion we tried to modernise it, making it a family day with games and quizzes. I remember the visiting missionary playing tennis with some youngsters during the afternoon.

We really tried our best over the first six years in the

parish. We adopted link missionaries, held meetings, used modern methods and literature. The huge effort was only slightly rewarded. On paper we were a 'missionary-minded church'. But in fact our overseas concern was more an optional interest maintained by a few enthusiasts. The only thing that did catch the church's enthusiasm was the appalling poverty in Uganda and Rwanda. We began to send parcels out to the church there. The local hospital gave us some obsolete equipment. The ladies knitted blankets. Members gave old sheets that could be made into bandages. We even sent empty yoghurt pots which were very useful out in these areas.

'Why is it', I asked myself in January 1982, 'that most aspects of the church seem to be developing and improving, but not the missionary interest. We've put a lot of effort into it. But I've got to be honest—it's not really working'. I shared my concern with others and we did what we always do when we're stuck—called an evening of prayer.

In the middle of February we met, prayed and shared. The whole event was inconclusive. Various suggestions were made but people were riding their hobby horses rather than hearing anything significant from the Lord. One person stressed the Muslim World but, no one seemed enthusiastic. I said I felt ministry to the Jews ought to figure in our concern. For a long time I had been doing extensive studies in the Old Testament. Both the historical books and, especially, the prophets had stimulated in me a quite deep interest in Israel past, present and future. This was what prompted my suggestion but it didn't meet with much interest. In spite of our praying and striving the Lord was not ready to speak to us about the matter of our overseas interests. But we took the vital step of 'laying down' all the present concerns for God to take away or give back as He chose.

107

Four months later we had another evening of prayer about mission. At this we sensed God was saying something which seemed quite radical to us. He drew our attention to Acts 1:8 'You will receive power when the Holy Spirit comes on you; and you will be my witnesses in Jerusalem, and in all Judea and Samaria, and to the ends of the earth'. It became clear that we were called to more than prayer interest and sending cheques to missionary societies. We were also to go to our 'Jerusalem' (Hawkwell); 'Judea' (Our Area); 'Samaria' (Our Nation) and the ends of the earth. We would have direct contact with the church in these various areas, including overseas, although we would still support missionary societies. We began to understand that there was no distinction between local evangelism and overseas mission. God was calling us to obey Acts 1:8. What that would mean in practice we did not at that time understand. Very soon afterwards, however, the Lord began to guide us about our overseas mission in a quite remarkable way. Here is how Patricia describes what happened:

'It was June 24th 1982. I remember distinctly that I was preparing a liver and bacon casserole for the evening meal. Not that such mundane things are normally etched on my memory, but what happened to me at that time made a deep impression. In the afternoon a church member had casually mentioned a Prayer for Israel meeting which she had attended in London. I registered interest as I had always had a vague concern for the Jews and wondered if we should be doing more as a church to serve them.

'An hour or so later, as I was busy in the kitchen, a sense of grief overwhelmed me. There was an experience of weeping deep within my spirit. No tears, no words, but a heart cry to God for His estranged people, the Jews. I continued my tasks only with difficulty—the

108

burden was so great. I knew enough to understand what it was that was happening within me. It was a form of intercession alluded to in Romans 8:26. "In the same way, the Spirit helps us in our weakness. We do not know what we ought to pray, but the Spirit Himself intercedes for us with groans that words cannot express." I had experienced it in this intensity only once before. Then it had been a depth of longing for creation itself to be set free from "its bondage to decay". No way can this form of prayer be worked up—it is just something which the Spirit gives as He chooses. This time it was for the Jews, for many to return to their land, for Israel to repent before the Lord, and for the Gentiles too that they would not also be cut off from God's mercy. Since that time I have heard of many throughout the world whom God has burdened in a similar way for Israel.

'I was supposed to go to a meeting that evening but I made an excuse to stay at home. I couldn't wait until the meal was over and I could get to be with the Lord on my own. I didn't quite know what to do about the burden I had been given, so I turned to the passage of scripture which I was due to read in my next Quiet Time. I started at 1 Chronicles 25 but my heart sank somewhat as I was confronted with lists of names! Even so there were gems to "read, mark, learn and inwardly digest". But I felt compelled to read on and on, into 2 Chronicles, until suddenly I knew the Lord was speaking directly to me from Solomon's prayer in 2 Chronicles 6:32–33. "As for the foreigner who does not belong to your people Israel but has come from a distant land because of your great name and mighty hand and your outstretched arm—when he comes and prays towards this temple, then hear from heaven your dwelling-place, and do whatever the foreigner asks of you, so that all the peoples of the earth may know your name and fear you, as do your own people Israel, and may know that this house that I have built bears your Name."

'I knew then that not only were we to pray for Israel but also to go there, and that through that obedience God would bless our outreach to Jew and Gentile alike.

'Next morning I was involved in a prayer group. We had been praying about matters far removed from Israel so I asked God to make it obvious if I should share my experience. Suddenly Jan Acton, one of the group members, blurted out that God had impressed on her and her husband, Pete, that His call to us as a church to be His witnesses, in Jerusalem, Judaea, Samaria and the uttermost parts, was not only to be taken metaphorically but also literally. At first Pete and Jan had wondered if God was saying that as a church we should make Israel a major prayer topic, but then they too sensed it would mean going as well as praying. In fact God had spoken to them through that very same verse: 2 Chronicles 6:32! In my diary for June 25th I wrote: "I am convinced this means that Israel will be the hub of our outreach, because it is the hub of God's purposes to bring all the peoples of the earth to know His name and fear Him."

'Then followed more prayer, sharing with the elders, conveying it all to the leaders and finally the whole church. Gradually almost the entire fellowship came to share this new aspect of our vision. Prayer groups were formed, links forged with "Prayer for Israel" and folks out in Israel, and the way opened up for various leaders, including ourselves, to make trips to Israel "to spy out the land".

'The prayer continued but only now is the way beginning to open up for close links to be cemented with folk serving God in Israel. The vision given over two years ago is about to become reality. But, interestingly, it was

110

only as it was pursued by faith that the rest of our outreach fell into place.' + can feed 5000 Africans (with 1000 fish?) John 14:12

10: Encounter with the Housechurches

'What I can't understand is how you can stay in the Church of England', remarked a lady after a united celebration in 1984. She had been Anglican but had left to join a Baptist Church. I was able to give her briefly a clear and definite answer. Had she asked me a year earlier I might have answered, 'I think we may well leave.'

Part of our concern in outreach was to be in touch with other churches for mutual encouragement. Over the years I had been invited to speak at renewal meetings and clergy gatherings locally and in other parts of the country. In 1979 and 1980 I led two Holiday Bible weeks for people from various denominations at Haldon Court, Exmouth. In 1981 I was asked to chair the S.E. Essex Charismatic Fraternal of Ministers. This consisted of Baptist, Elim and other Free church ministers as well as Chris Chilvers the leader of the local housechurch. In fact, we met in Chris' home.

Until then I had taken little notice of the housechurch movement. I had heard that they encouraged people to leave their churches and that they were sometimes unbalanced in their beliefs and practice. In the seventies I had become involved with an ecumenical team who organised monthly renewal meetings in Southend. Chris was also involved and I vaguely picked up from others that there had been some hurts in the past over the housechurch movement. However, I took to Chris on first meeting him and the friendship developed. The two of us met on a few occasions privately as well as in the Fraternal.

I began to realise that there was some suspicion of the housechurch movement in the Fraternal too. This made me uneasy but I have always been one to expose myself sympathetically to what others are teaching even if I found it challenging and disturbing.

In June 1981 the Southend Christian Fellowship, the local housechurch, arranged three public meetings at which Arthur Wallis was to speak. He is a leader in the Bradford/Dales Bible Week strand of the movement. I had very mixed feelings about this. I wanted to hear him but I expected he would be calling us to leave our denominations. Because of my deep longing to obey the Lord, come what may, and my unhappiness about certain wrong things in the Church of England, I found the prospect of this meeting rather threatening. In the end I decided that I should go but I didn't announce the meetings to the church. I didn't want to lose some of my best folk to the housechurches!

I attended the meetings and sat there very up-tight, just waiting for the 'leave your denominations' message. It never came. In fact, Arthur said at one point that to continue in obedience to God would mean for some, leaving their denominational church but for others it would not. Many of my prejudices and suspicions began to disappear. I was surprised, however, to find that some of my colleagues in the Fraternal had 'heard' Arthur Wallis tell everyone to leave their denominations in those meetings—more a comment on the power of prejudice than accurate hearing.

The following month a friend came to stay for a few days. He was at one time an Anglican incumbent but had left the Church of England largely over the issue of

Baptism. He is older than me and has a very helpful counselling and teaching ministry for which I have great respect. One morning he said to me, 'You know, Tony, the number of churches in the historic denominations which have gone on to the second stage of renewal (renewal of structures) is very few and far between. You will eventually reach a "denominational ceiling". The present renewal movement is meant to affect the denominations deeply but God will not renew them as such. The existence of denominations is contrary to his will. The time will come when we have to leave them—or be thrown out.'

I did not want to hear this. I was becoming very unhappy about the doctrinal and moral confusion in the Church of England. I knew deep down, and still do, that if ever obedience to the Lord meant leaving the Anglican Church, I would do so. But I hoped very much it would not be necessary. My contacts with Chris and Arthur Wallis had proved disturbing. It was all a bit too much. My friend went on to say that in his counselling work he had had to set people free from spiritual bondage to Anglicanism. Some people had been unable to see certain truths or to take certain steps of obedience until they had received prayer for deliverance. He felt it was quite possible for denominationalism to be a spiritual, even demonic, bondage. Knowing that my friend was far from being one of those unbalanced people who see demons lurking everywhere, I found these comments disturbing but interesting. With four years more experience, I believe there is truth in what he said about this bondage.

Throughout the summer this conflict about leaving denominations was in my thoughts. In September Patricia and I went to the first National Anglican Renewal Ministries Conference at Swanwick, wondering exactly how we would react to it. Looked at objectively,

114

it was a very good conference. The teaching was good and seeing all those Anglicans 'lost in wonder, love and praise' was quite exciting. But our thoughts and feelings were in turmoil. 'Was renewal in the Anglican Church really a dead end? Would renewed Anglicans have to pull out or would they just accept second best and lose their blessing in the end? Would they go on to the second stage of renewal i.e. Renewal of Structures? Or would renewal be contained and eventually stifled by traditional Anglican structures?' The presence of another friend who was about to leave the Anglican ministry didn't exactly help my peace of mind either. The happier the conference members became, the more miserable we felt.

One afternoon I had to take the car to the garage. I was a little late in returning and simply couldn't find the discussion group to which I was assigned. So I returned to my room and got out Arthur Wallis' book 'The Radical Christian'. I looked at the cover: 'Will this be it?' I thought. 'Will this book finally convince me that God is calling me out of the Church of England? Perhaps I shouldn't read it.' But I knew I could never live with such a cowardly decision. I read the book and found I agreed with most of it. But I felt that possibly the principles taught in it might be worked out in an Anglican context.

Back in Essex the Fraternal seemed to be going well. The level of commitment was deepening and we seemed to have a more mature attitude to the 'housechurch' issue. At the end of January 1982 the Fraternal arranged a public meeting in Emmanuel entitled 'Together for Celebration and Vision.' Some 350 people from over 10 churches attended. I shared in some detail our vision for the church in the area and a Baptist pastor preached. Three people committed their lives to Christ, several were healed and a number experienced Renewal in the Spirit. There were a few imperfections. As someone put

it, there were those there who laboured under the misap-
prehension that the Lord was deaf! The noise was a bit
much for others. There was a public message in tongues
which we weren't happy about. But all in all it was a
good evening.

By this time, Chris Chilvers and I knew one another
well enough to relax about our differences. We could
joke together about his hope that I would leave the
Church of England or about the faults (real and
rumoured) in our two churches. Consequently when he
invited me to attend a 3-day Ministers Conference at the
headquarters of their churches in Bradford, I was not at
all threatened. On the contrary, I looked forward to it.

So on March 15th 1982, with the pastor of a local
Evangelical Church, we drove up north. We spent the
journey discussing the housechurch movement's
approach in some depth. I felt a sort of excitement mixed
with a desire to be wide open and vulnerable to anything
God had to say to me during the conference. On the first
evening we attended a large evangelistic celebration in a
hall at Bradford University. Many hundreds of people
from housechurches in the area had gathered, bringing
unbelievers with them. Bryn Jones preached a simple
but powerful evangelistic message and many responded
to the invitation. This event and subsequent experiences
have made me realise how unfair is the sweeping general-
isation that housechurches are inward looking and not
involved in evangelism. It is not true of Southend Christian Fellowship, which is heavily involved in outreach.

I found the conference stimulating and helpful. There
was nothing unbalanced or unbiblical in the teaching,
yet controversial areas were not avoided. The overall
leaders are clearly men of God with a deep desire for
Christ to be honoured and His Kingdom extended. We
were treated very graciously and, in no sense, was any
pressure brought to bear on any matter including the

116

denominational issue. Personal contact with the hundred or so people present—ministers from various denominations as well as housechurches, proved very fruitful. The breakdown of my prejudices which had begun in June 1981, was completed at this conference.

One interesting incident took place in a small fellowship group to which I was assigned one afternoon and it was to do with the ministry of women. Patricia and I had met at London Bible College, where we were both reading for a degree in theology. We attended lectures together, studied together and held hands together—concealed by our academic gowns—in chapel! Before we met, we both knew God had called us to full-time Christian work. Subsequently, we both felt we were called together into the Anglican Ministry. We had a growing conviction that God had given us one ministry which we both shared. We can, and do, minister separately but our ministry is greatly enriched by each other. All this had been confirmed by mature counsellors as well as by the parish leadership.

Nevertheless, my reading of the New Testament leads me inescapably to the conclusion that the norm is for the overall leadership in the church to be male. Patricia agrees with this, as do the other prominent women in the parish. But the two of us, individually and together, have spent much time in prayer and heartsearching as to whether we have the balance right or not. Certainly I am strongly against women being treated as inferior or relegated to doing only mundane duties in the church. So in Hawkwell the elders regularly pray and discuss matters with their wives whilst making and accepting responsibility for the decisions. All the housegroup leaders are couples and we believe it is vital for couples to minister together where possible.

I was still working through this matter when I went to Bradford. From what I had heard, the housechurches had a 'down' on women. I was to be very surprised in that little afternoon fellowship group. We began to pray for each other under the leadership of David Matthew, editor of 'Restoration' magazine. Now David hardly knew me. If he knew I was married he certainly knew nothing of Patricia or of the questions we had been facing. But when my turn came to be prayed for, he had a prophecy for me, which quite staggered me. 'You are to listen to your wife', he said, 'for she has wisdom to correct your convictions.'

Later in the year, we invited David Mansell and Bryn Jones to speak to the Fraternal. Unfortunately again certain of the members 'heard' them say what they did not, in fact, say i.e. 'leave your denominations.' On the contrary, they had agreed that for some it would be right to stay in the historic denominations, so long as it was consistent with obedience to the Lord. At one public meeting in our area, addressed by Bryn, I was the only 'non-housechurch' leader on the platform. I felt welcome and at home. I preached at Southend Christian Fellowship in December 1982 and Chris Chilvers preached at Emmanuel a month later.

During 1983 I felt we might have to leave the Church of England because of its doctrinal and moral confusion. But I was not at all sure that if we did so, we would link up with any housechurch strand. I shared this with Chris and we got into a discussion about the Ephesian's four leading ministries—apostles, prophets, evangelists, pastors and teachers. I see no justification for the opinion of those who say these ministries are irrelevant to today's church. Perhaps the most controversial one is the apostolic ministry. Clearly there are today no apostles on a level with the Twelve or Paul—witnesses of the Resurrection and inspired writers of Scripture. Modern apostolic ministries are subject to scripture. But such ministries do exist. Some men have the ability to plant and

118

build churches. They are capable of fulfilling this ministry on a non-local basis and of standing with and encouraging other men who perhaps do not have an apostolic gift. Such a ministry is clearly recognised and organised in The Dales housechurch strand. But I believe it is present in the historic denominations even if it is not always so clearly recognised and organised. These denominations may well not be truly structured charismatically. Consequently, men who are officially in an apostolic position may not always have the spiritual gift of an apostolic ministry in the biblical sense. But it is possible for those in historic denominations to benefit from a genuine apostolic ministry if they so wish. It is also important for those with apostolic gifts to relate to one another for mutual benefit and, sometimes, correction. Any apostolic ministry should not be a heavy 'covering'. Rather it should liberate the local church, encouraging its growth to maturity.

During 1984 on several occasions, I met up with another strand of the movement—John Noble and his team from Romford. They have a rather more relaxed approach than the Dales strand, especially concerning authority. It is also clear that they have a genuine desire to relate to Christians in other denominations without encouraging people to leave their existing churches.

I am convinced that we in the historic denominations must listen carefully to what the housechurches are saying. It is not good enough to feel threatened by them and so to dismiss them on the basis of prejudice. The movement is, I believe, initiated by God and, whatever its imperfections, has much to teach us. True there are housechurches and housechurches. But then there are parish churches and parish churches! Some individuals, even some groups, will be unbalanced. There are those that have become cults. But these extremes do not invalidate the whole movement.

It is clear that some unbalanced church members will go off to find anything new. Also, some housechurch members might urge members of other denominations to join them. But generally speaking people leave our churches for housechurches because they are not finding the life, fellowship, worship and ministry they are looking for. It's an easy excuse to blame the housechurches. But I don't think we shall lose people if we really have the courage to embrace and obey all that the Holy Spirit is doing today. The existence of the housechurch movement is largely an indictment of those of us in the historic denominations. In many cases the ecclesiastical 'wineskins' have proved largely or wholly inflexible, and so the new wine of the Spirit has inevitably split them. Some historic denominational churches are so dead or unbiblical that Christians staying in them out of a misguided loyalty are being harmed.

We sometimes forget, it seems, that Satan is 'the Father of lies' who delights in spreading rumour and gossip. Sadly some Christians, even Christian leaders, readily co-operate with him. Many false stories circulate about the housechurches. Interestingly, some of them circulate about Hawkwell too. When someone becomes disenchanted with a church, especially if an unsuccessful attempt has been made to correct some serious error in his life, he can become embittered. This doesn't happen in every case. But some such people begin a personal crusade of vitriolic and wildly unbalanced criticisms against the fellowship they have left. Unfortunately, human nature being what it is, there is no lack of people in other churches who readily believe such stories, especially if they are somewhat critical to begin with. Seldom is the basic rule about hearing both sides of the story adhered to.

Favourite rumours about housechurches are that they exercise a very heavy authority and require unquestioning obedience. They only want 'yes-men'. They only collect people from other churches and don't evangelise. They're all froth and there's no solid teaching etc. I'm not saying that there is never any truth in these criticisms. But we need at least to check the truth and to be aware of the power of gossip and prejudice especially when we feel threatened.

However, I believe the housechurches have lessons to learn too. Church history proves that all 'break-away' groups become denominations and then fossilise. I genuinely hope that this will never happen to the housechurch movement, but I fear it has begun in some cases. Secondly, God hasn't given up on the historic denominations yet. Some of us are called to obey him within them even when we share many convictions with the housechurches. Thirdly, it is a known fact that a man's followers may be more hard-line than he is. For example some local groups may be more authoritarian than national leadership would ever be. (In Hawkwell we have on one or two occasions, discovered that a leader or member has held what the elders consider to be too heavy a view of authority. This may have led on the one hand to an authoritarian action or to a person being afraid to express disagreement. In either case, we have ensured the error is corrected). Fourthly, every Christian group which has met more than once has traditions. Tradition is not wrong. It can even be helpful so long as it is biblical and flexible in the Spirit's hands. We in the historic denominations may sometimes feel our traditions are irksome. But at least they have the value of forcing us to think through our new, radical ideas more than we may do if we left the denominations to start afresh. In order to obey God we may sometimes have to forsake a particular tradition. But we ought to be careful and prayerful before doing so. There are housechurch leaders who cannot write an article without criticising tradition. In a strange way they are in bondage. They feel bound to discard tradition simply because it is tradition, whether it is helpful or not. That is as bad as maintaining tradition for its own sake.

11: Discipline in Intercession

One dark evening recently I hurried up to Emmanuel to do some urgent photocopying. Some lights were on in the church and as I approached the door of the vestry, which housed the photocopier, I could hear voices. I stopped and immediately could tell that a group of men were praying together in the vestry. My plan to photocopy was abandoned, but I drove away, quietly praising God for the spirit of prayer he had given us as a church. In fact, there are so many prayercells now I can't remember when they all meet. It was not always like that.

One of my vivid childhood memories is about a prayer meeting. My father used to lead a Saturday evening prayer meeting at the little chapel which he and my mother still attend. One Saturday I sensed all was not well concerning this prayer meeting so I decided, for the first time, to accompany him and give him moral support. We were silent together—just the two of us—in the chapel waiting for others to come. Nobody came. That night I saw my father weep in that chapel. He wept because he knew the power of prayer but the church was neglecting it. This experience had a profound effect on me and stayed in the back of my mind over the years.

During my teenage years we attended another church. I sometimes went to the Wednesday prayer meeting. I'll never forget how boring it was gazing in the silences at the tattered vestry carpet, listening to the hissing gas fire and the occasional stomach rumble. But I used to feel

123

very virtuous after it had finished—having endured such an ordeal yet again. I'm afraid that many of my experiences of evangelical prayer meetings over the years have been singularly uninspiring. Little wonder that I sense a lack of emphasis on prayer in some evangelical circles, a fact that grieves me almost as much as it did my father on that Saturday evening so many years ago.

It was my experience of the Baptism in the Spirit that opened my eyes to the reality of prayer. And this happened many years after my definite conversion experience. I am sure that Baptism in the Spirit is really part of conversion. A person cannot be born again without receiving the Spirit. And the Spirit cannot be only partially present. But the problem is that, like me, many Christians don't experience the fullness of the power of the Spirit promised to them. This power is part of the birthright of every Christian and should be experienced at conversion. But because of lack of teaching or lack of faith it is often only partially experienced. So I am happy to pray for a person to be baptised in the Holy Spirit, i.e. to experience the fullness of power of the Spirit they received at conversion. For many prayer with the laying on of hands is a very important stimulus to faith. Through it, the Spirit is released in them. The norm should be that we experience all this at conversion. But if we haven't done so, we need to be practical and ask the Lord to release the experience of the Baptism in the Spirit and the gifts of the Spirit in us.

Early in 1967 I was in my final year at Oak Hill Theological College. In a few months time I would be thrust upon some unsuspecting parish as a curate. The college laid heavy emphasis on the Quiet Time—a period of private prayer each morning. I have to confess that in spite of all my evangelical background, training and experience I was finding prayer a bore. Bible reading wasn't much better. My spiritual life seemed to have dried up. For too long I had been dealing with holy things from an academic point of view.

One particularly exquisite form of torture encouraged at the college was student prayer partnerships. Every week a list was pinned on the board. Each student was paired off with another and the two were expected to meet for prayer during the week. My defence strategy was to develop a bad memory and not actually to get round to meeting my partner. Fairly often this worked—maybe others felt the same way! One week, however, it didn't. I met up with one of the students whom I had heard was one of these strange charismatics. Until then, I had taken no interest in charismatic renewal. But somehow I felt this student might be able to help me. Uncharacteristically, I unburdened myself to him, telling him how bad things were spiritually. I was encouraged by the chat—the first of several.

At half term Patricia and I accepted this student's invitation to spend a long weekend at St. Mark's, Gillingham, which had recently been transformed by charismatic renewal. We liked what we saw. On the Monday evening after reading about the work of the Spirit in the Book of Acts, we accepted an offer by the lay reader and the curate to have prayer so that we might experience the Baptism in the Spirit. They took Patricia off into another room leaving me alone in the vicarage kitchen. Eventually, they burst back into the room and told me Patricia had had a wonderful experience of God and was speaking in tongues. 'Oh no,' I thought, 'now I'm married to a nutcase. It'll never happen to me.' The two men prayed for me at length whilst I studied the plastic tablecloth. The more they prayed, the worse I felt. It would never happen. Eventually they stopped and said, 'Don't worry. Just believe it's happened and you will experience it.' I thought that was a polite way of saying they were fed up with praying.

Disappointed I began to collect our cases to return to London. And I relaxed! It was then that it hit me. I was almost bowled over by a sense of God's love, power and greatness. On the train I couldn't stop grinning in a dazed sort of way, much to the amusement of my student friend. In the weeks that followed, I found I wanted to pray continuously, and particularly to praise God. We met in prayer groups and had some really wonderful times. What a contrast!

Six months later, because we allowed lack of love towards certain people to creep into our lives, we began to 'go off' renewal. We could never deny the blessing we had received but we did not know how to go on from it. Our prayer life began to deteriorate, until for long periods in my first curacy and the early months of my second, I wasn't really praying at all. I was if anything, in a worse state than I had been in early 1967. It was only after we re-entered renewal in 1972 that our prayer life improved, both individually and corporately.

At the time I was curate at St. Barnabas, Cheltenham. During 1972 we began to have an early evening hour of prayer each week. The atmosphere was so different from what we had previously experienced in Cheltenham. The prayer was deep and spontaneous. It seemed to flow in harmony. It was exciting. We didn't want to stop and couldn't wait to meet again. There were many answers to prayer and the Lord did a great work of renewal in the church in the early seventies.

We had similar experiences when we moved to Hawkwell in 1975. In the early years whenever there seemed to be a need, we called an evening of prayer and they were just like those Cheltenham meetings. In September 1975 we started Prayer Breakfasts at 7.00 am on Saturdays. In April 1978 we began an hour of prayer at 8.00 am on Sundays initially to pray for a series of sermons on 'The Holy Spirit in the Church'. They were good times.

In July 1978 we met to discuss our ailing Evangelism Programme. Quite unexpectedly we felt God was calling us to arrange a weekly Parish Day of Prayer. Two months later this began. Each Thursday a number of us met for an hour of prayer at 6.30 am. At 9.15 am two other groups met, one at each end of the parish. A small group met at 12.30 pm. We began to publish a Prayer News sheet each Sunday which recorded answers to prayer and suggested new prayer topics. I really believe that the present exciting phase of God's work in Hawkwell began at that time through that prayer.

From March 1979 we added an early evening hour of prayer for the nation and this led us to an ever deepening concern for the situation in Britain and for international affairs. Occasionally, we gave the day of prayer a special emphasis. For example in the first week of September 1979 we made the major emphasis the new spontaneous evening worship service. Seven weeks later we concentrated on prayer for a deeper renewal by the Holy Spirit within the parish.

In the Spring of 1980, we heard of a set of tapes on intercession by a lady called Joy Dawson. There is a right time to hear a particular aspect of Christian teaching. Before that time the message is either interesting but irrelevant or even discouraging. It was just the right time for us to hear those tapes. They opened our eyes to a new depth of intercession which involved 'hearing' from God what to pray and entering into 'spiritual warfare' in prayer.

At the same time we heard of a day conference being held in our area by the Lydia Fellowship. This organisation was set up to teach women about intercession and to train them to intercede. It encourages the formation of

127

prayer cells and holds national and regional conferences. Some of our women attended this local conference and returned excited about what they had experienced. The literature they brought back helped move us deeper into intercession. With the church's backing, a fortnightly Lydia group was set up. It tended to become a pioneer group exploring greater depths than other prayer groups in the parish. We ensured that what was learnt by the Lydia prayer cell was conveyed to the church leadership and so to the rest of the praying members.

By November 1981 we sensed that new developments in the Church's prayer life were called for. So we arranged an evening of prayer about Parish Prayer life. At that time in addition to the weekly day of prayer and the fortnightly Lydia group there was prayer for worship before the evening services and for an hour on Monday, a fortnightly evening of prayer for the nation and various other prayer times. We also had a Prayer Partnership scheme which encouraged married couples to meet as a foursome, or two individuals of the same sex to meet for prayer each week. The main recommendation to arise from this special evening of prayer was that the more experienced intercessors from the Lydia Group should each lead a prayer cell. These cells would grow and divide and each major on a specific area of concern.

Three months later the new pattern began with one early morning prayer cell, three morning prayer cells at Emmanuel and one at St. Mary's, replacing the original Thursday morning groups. There was also one Friday evening cell. The leaders of the cells met weekly in what had been the Lydia Group. When a cell had more than seven members, it divided. In order to ensure a depth of disciplined intercession in the cells the elders were very careful about the appointment of leaders.

By May 1982 there were twelve prayer cells. Most of them concentrated on an area of parish life which they believed to be their special calling, but many other topics were prayed about. We encouraged them not to pray about personal concerns which we felt would better be dealt with in the housegroups. Occasionally we called the prayer cells together for sharing, training or special prayer.

Later in the year we began to feel strongly that intercession should not be seen as an optional activity for the 80 members who happened to be keen on it. Rather it was as necessary for the whole membership as, for example say, fellowship. We therefore asked the housegroups to spend at least one meeting each month in intercession. Some of the members would be inexperienced in, or even apprehensive of, intercession so we ensured that each group contained an experienced intercessor to lead the group's evenings of prayer. In addition to local church needs each group was asked to pray about wider issues such as our outreach interests.

We asked each group to pray about the personal needs of its members on other occasions. There is always a grave danger of intercession groups turning in on themselves so we laboured the point about being outward looking. Patricia wrote in 'Focus' (as we now call our weekly prayer-news sheet), 'At first you will perhaps find it a bit daunting but gradually you will discover that there can be real excitement in praying together, especially when you begin to get answers. . . . Many of us can testify to a significant growth in our spiritual lives as we come together, not for our own benefit, but to give ourselves in sacrificial prayer for others. We have discovered that the principle 'It is in giving that you receive' actually works! So why not try it for yourself?' Over the following months the housegroup members discovered that she was right.

The prayer cells developed, plus regular evenings devoted to prayer for outreach, for Israel, for the nation and world. Also every leader and worker in the church met regularly for prayer not only all together in the monthly Leaders' Fellowship but also in sectional groups e.g. youthleaders. It became clear that the evenings were overloaded with meetings—especially prayer cells. So by the end of 1983 we began to move cells to the early morning for those working and in the daytime for those not in employment. As part of this process, we asked the housegroups now to have two evenings per month devoted to intercession—one about our church and local outreach; the other about the nation and one of our overseas concerns.

By the end of 1984 there were 18 weekly prayer cells involving about 110 churchmembers. Four of the cells meet in the early morning and two in the evening. The rest meet mid-morning, most of them on Thursday so that creche facilities can be provided. Since so many churchmembers are involved in prayer cells, we no longer ask the housegroups to have two evenings of inter-cession a month. The message has got across that every member should be involved in intercession. They have a vision and enthusiasm for it and new members quickly come to share this. We turn some of the Evening Praise services over to intercession and hold midweek evenings of prayer for outreach. Each housegroup has a monthly evening of intercession.

There is a big difference between real intercession and many traditional 'prayer meetings'. We encourage members to prepare themselves spiritually before they come to the cell. They may well therefore receive some-thing beforehand from the Lord which they can bring to share at the meeting. Let's look at a typical prayer cell. They pray for parish evangelism and normally about half a dozen members meet weekly. In the first few minutes they look back at the evangelistic Guest Service last Sunday. It was led by the Young Church with children taking the prayers and the teenagers singing and doing a drama. There was no visible response to the invitation but later in the day a married couple committed their lives to Christ as a result. The sense of gratitude is soon turned into praise. A joyful song of thanksgiving is followed by two quieter worship songs which help the group to concentrate on the greatness, holiness and love of God. This leads naturally to prayers of confession of the members' unworthiness before God. At a suitable moment the leader speaks whilst the group remains in prayer. He leads them in giving their own ideas, interests and worries over to God so that they will not hinder the prayer. He then leads them in asking for the Holy Spirit to fill them and to give them His wisdom. Finally, he reminds the group of the Cross and Resurrection in which Jesus defeated all the powers of sin, death and hell. So the members realise afresh the protection and spiritual authority this affords them. Satan's messengers will not deflect them or defeat them as they seek to fulfil God's purpose in intercession.

Briefly specific prayer needs are shared. The Christmas leaflet will soon be distributed to every house and final plans for evangelism over the festive season will soon be made. Having shared these and other evangelistic needs the leader asks the Lord to impress upon the group what He wants them to emphasise in prayer, even if it cuts across what they anticipate. So the prayers begin for the Christmas outreach. There is nothing wrong with the prayers but somehow they lack depth and intensity. Then someone shares that he feels they should pray for families where only one family member attends church. In particular, he feels the group should pray for those who don't attend. The leader checks with the other people present and there is a sense of agreement and enthusiasm about this subject, even though they hadn't planned to pray in this way.

One after another, the cell members pray with feeling on this subject. They don't worry about repetition. This is a battle for people to come to belief so the prayers are directed against unbelief, or circumstances preventing them coming to faith. All the prayers are to the point so the leader doesn't on this occasion, have to guide them back to the subject. The members feel an inner 'burden' in their spirits about the prayer topic and they continue to pray until this 'burden' lifts. At one point they felt together that they had the authority to 'bind' the spiritual forces of unbelief over certain individuals they were praying for. Two people believed they had a prophetic word of encouragement. One of these messages spoke movingly about God's great love for the people they were praying for. Another spoke of the need for members to meet socially the people for whom they were praying, so that barriers and fears could be broken down. Maybe something should be done through the housegroups. The leader wrote this second message down so that it could be passed on to the elders for their prayers and possible action.

The hour simply flashed by and, all too soon, the members had to disperse and go off to work. It was a good start to the day. The cells aren't always as good as that but often they are. With 18 weekly cells a good deal of information is passed back to the elders who weigh it up prayerfully and, if necessary initiate action—through the PCC if it is a major issue. The PCC members are involved in prayer cells so they too take a mature and prayerful approach to what is put to them. Sometimes the elders ask the prayer cells (or the leaders) to pray through a particular topic and report back. Often the matter will then be shared in the Leaders' Fellowship. So by the time it reaches the PCC it has been very fully considered and prayed about—including by PCC members.

The legally established procedures of the Church of England are largely based on the idea of democracy and we respect that. However, we are seeking to go beyond that to what has been called 'theocracy'. By this we mean that we encourage members to grow in spirituality and prayerfulness so that they become sensitive to what the Spirit is saying to our church. They learn to 'hear' God, perhaps through scripture, or prophecy or by an inner conviction. This needs to be tested by reference to the others in leadership. But the end result is that we regularly come to unanimous conclusions. We are often genuinely able to say 'It seemed good to the Holy Spirit and to us that we should do this . . .'. That does not mean there is no debate or no opportunity for questions and disagreement. That would be wrong and dangerous. But increasingly, as we become more sensitive to the Holy Spirit the convictions and decisions are unanimous. This is often the case now in the PCC.

Sometimes people outside the church think that this unanimity is achieved by a heavy authority which crushes dissent or by the leaders being 'yes-men'. In fact, nothing could be further from the truth. I thank God that I am surrounded by men and women who are sufficiently in touch with God spiritually that they would correct me (and have corrected me) when I get something wrong. I trust their corporate discernment. It is an invaluable asset especially when we sail in uncharted waters.

I used to react inwardly against people who constantly say 'The Lord told me this' or 'The Lord spoke to me'. After all, even as a clergyman, I didn't think I 'heard' God like that. Part of me wanted to, the other part thought these people were indulging in wishful thinking. In some cases I believe they were. Certainly any such alleged message from God needs to be checked. Is it biblical? Do other mature Christians agree? Nevertheless, God can 'speak' to us, not only through scripture, but through prophecy or through an inner conviction etc. Some of us who are more sophisticated—especially those trained in theology—need to become more humble and open to such things in a childlike way. But it will always be an act of faith. We need to recognise the 'voice' of God and to have the courage to check it out with others. This is vital in intercession.

On the very first Parish Day of Prayer in September 1978 one of our members felt a strong urge to pray for the Pope—not a regular topic in our prayers in Hawkwell. This was, in fact, the day before Pope John Paul I suddenly died and so the prayer was specially appropriate.

In August 1980, during an Evening Praise Service, we quite unexpectedly felt we had to pray for Poland. This was very unusual because at that stage there was little emphasis on intercession in Evening Praise and I can't remember our praying for Poland previously. We heard afterwards that the Polish Government had suddenly resigned.

In 1981 the Lord on one occasion gave a prayer cell a burden to pray for the Maze Prison in Northern Ireland. The subject seemed impossibly large. As they began to pray they sensed an oppressive heaviness and darkness. Someone had a mental picture of the prison covered with a thick grey blanket. It seemed impossible for this to be penetrated with the light of God's love. The person then prayed that God would send an angel to lift up the corner of the blanket. They prayed for a Christian from outside the prison to visit and witness effectively to Christ. Many months later, we learned that this had happened and that a hardened I.R.A. criminal had been converted, which had led on to a deep work by the Holy Spirit in the prison. It was so encouraging to know that our prayers, which God had so specifically inspired, were used along with the prayers of no doubt many others in this matter.

Intercession is a dialogue. We can learn to 'hear' God and he will inform and direct our prayers. Given such sensitivity and persistent, believing prayer, intercession is the most powerful spiritual force available to us.

handy in ending slave trade + Inquisition sooner?

12: Standing Together

'What is this vision you keep talking about? I don't know what you mean.' The questioner was an influential church member who was rather critical of the way things were going in the church. The occasion was a Leaders' Fellowship in 1981 and the other leaders looked at me expecting some neat, pre-packaged answer. I realised I couldn't give an adequate answer. What was our vision as a church? Just exactly what were we aiming at? I knew vaguely but I'd never sat down and organised my thoughts on this vital matter, let alone put them on paper. 'That's a good question', I replied. 'I can't give you a proper answer just like that. But I will try to put some thoughts down on paper as soon as possible, and let everyone have a copy.'

For some time I had been giving teaching on the importance of unity within the local church if it was to fulfil its mission. It was the depth of unity the New Testament demanded that had challenged me so deeply. For months I had been unable to get some verses from John 17 out of my mind. Jesus prayed (v 21–23) 'That all of them may be one, Father, just as you are in me and I am in you . . . that they may be one as we are one. . . . May they be brought to complete unity to let the world know that you sent me and have loved them even as you have loved me.'

Why hadn't I seen it before? Here was no vague ecumenical unity, still less the loose collection of independent individuals one finds in some churches. Jesus was praying for a unity so complete that it was comparable to the Unity in the Trinity. Then the world would believe. I coined the phrase 'evangelistic unity' and realised the local church had to work for its own unity before it sought to relate in depth to believers in other denominations. Then I began to notice other statements in the New Testament like 'All the believers were one in heart and mind' (Acts 4:32). Paul prays that the church will have such a spirit of unity that it may glorify God with 'one heart and mouth' (Rom. 15:5–6). The New Testament, therefore, calls for a church to be one in conviction, feeling, understanding and profession. It is to be a closely knit body in which the members 'belong to one another' (Romans 12:4–5; Ephesians 4:15–16, 25). They are to be bound together in a Christ-like love (John 13:34–35; 15:12–13) and to lay down their lives for one another (1 John 3:16).

I began to contrast this teaching with the realities of the church today. Because we arc the national church we Anglicans sometimes seem suspicious of, or even antagonistic towards, a strong fellowship within the local church. We are afraid of becoming an exclusive sect. We value our parochial system whereby potentially we cater for everyone in the country. I feel as strongly as anyone that we must not become an exclusive, inward-looking sect. Rather we must put every effort into reaching the whole parish. But will this mission be achieved by a church which is run as a voluntary organisation whose main aim is to dispense spiritual benefits, like a spiritual wing of the Welfare State, to anyone who cares to visit it, without making any demands on that person? I cannot believe that Jesus, in his prayer in John 17, had such a church in mind. He prayed not for a loose collection of friendly folk who regard themselves as Christians but for a completely united, deeply committed fellowship. The rest of the New Testament speaks of such fellowship.

Jesus in his prayer said that the world would believe when they saw such unity.

The more I thought about it, the more I realised I was not at liberty to ignore Jesus' prayer and the New Testament teaching. We must aim at a completely united, deeply committed fellowship in Hawkwell whilst avoiding exclusivism and an inward-looking selfishness. If the Lord said in his prayer that this sort of fellowship would encourage the world to believe, who was I to disagree? The way of human wisdom may say 'Be nice to everyone. Make it easy for them. Don't make demands on them. That's the way to win them.' But the way of faith says, 'Follow the New Testament teaching. Encourage a strong fellowship. Reach out with the love and challenge of the Gospel. That's the way to win them.' In Hawkwell we are committed to this latter method.

So I was faced with two questions. How could we encourage the development of a fellowship which was 'one in heart and mind'? And how could we at the same time effectively reach out with the love of God to the whole parish, fulfilling our distinctive responsibility as a parish church?

If we were going to be 'one in heart and mind' we would need to have a united vision of the nature and mission of the local church. So I began to write down the vision I had and sensed many other people in the church had, even though it had never been previously organised into a coherent statement.* Initially, I just put it out informally to the leaders. Before we appointed elders, I put the statement out to the members to help them decide which men could further this vision of the church. By early 1982, though, we had begun to realise we must take steps to teach this vision systematically to

* see appendix

138

the membership, so that we could encourage an intelligent and whole-hearted commitment to it.

Consequently on March 8th 1982, the PCC approved the description of our vision of the nature and mission of the local church which I had produced a year earlier. They also agreed that we should teach the full biblical basis of the vision to all the members who were interested. But we also needed to know at the end of the course whether people did whole-heartedly agree with it or not. Was this a vision they could share? Could they commit themselves to working towards it? So the council decided that, after the teaching course, members should be asked for their reactions and invited to commit themselves specifically and definitely to the vision.

I drew up a systematic Bible Study Course based on the vision and for the rest of 1982 nearly all of the adult churchmembers worked through it in housegroups. The Leaders' Fellowship—approximately 40 leaders—expressed their whole-hearted agreement to the vision in the Spring. But the crunch would be the reaction of the membership. A good deal of individual help was given in addition to the teaching groups. It was important that the questions of each member were answered and that no-one misunderstood or felt pressurised. Eventually, we set Sunday January 9th 1983 as Commitment Sunday. How many would not only agree to the vision but also commit themselves actively to work towards it? In the event 129 adult members expressed a definite commitment to the vision during the special service that morning.

Meanwhile, we had been seriously considering how we could best fulfil the vision in practical terms. We concluded that housegroups would be a vital factor, both in maintaining fellowship and in reaching the approximately 10,000 parishioners. We decided that the housegroup system should be re-organised and expanded. As far as possible, we would gather together in each group people from a particular geographical area in the parish. Each group would then have responsibility in co-operation with the elders, to reach out pastorally and evangelistically to its own mini-parish, which was clearly defined for it. We decided to make this major alteration immediately after Commitment Sunday. This was logical since the new housegroups would be a major aid in the fulfilment of the vision.

However, we wanted to be thoroughly charismatic in our pattern of groups. We envisaged each group having a leadership team. It would have, in addition to the host, an overall leader, a teacher, a pastor (to oversee the pastoring of the group members and of local parishioners outside the group), an intercessor (to oversee the group's prayer life), an evangelist (to spearhead the group's evangelism) an administrator and a social organiser. Occasionally people 'wore two hats', e.g. the leader may also be the teacher, and we seemed short on evangelists at that stage. We have found it difficult to be strictly geographical for a variety of practical reasons. But the whole parish is divided into ten housegroup areas. In order to make the system work we have to assign people to various groups, otherwise we couldn't maintain a balance in the numbers, between the sexes, or of people with different gifts in each group. However if, as has happened several times, someone has problems with the way we have assigned them we try to fit in with their wishes.

During the first year of this new pattern of housegroups every home in the parish was visited at least once and literature was distributed three times to the whole parish. Various coffee mornings, book parties and pre-Christmas 'Open Home' evenings were also held. In addition to this there were a large number of special visits to the bereaved, those requesting baptism, people

140

moving into the area or those in need. For example, during a six week period in the summer all the housegroups provided a rota of two people five nights a week to take an elderly lady (not a churchmember) to see her husband in hospital.

Each housegroup also contributes to the welfare of the whole church. All the normal practical jobs—cleaning, grounds maintenance, flower rota, crèche, social events—are done by the housegroups on a rota basis. This means that everyone is involved, not simply a hard-pressed and, at times, resentful few. Once a month a different housegroup will plan and lead a special morning service at Emmanuel. They spend many hours planning and rehearsing. Normally the service includes drama and/or movement, testimony as well as all the usual elements. Sometimes I have been able to sit in the congregation and I've been thrilled to see the standard and the spiritual power of the group's work. Some groups have given an invitation at the end for those wanting to commit their life to Christ or have prayer for healing at the rail. On more than one occasion the response has exceeded that in many Guest Services which I have led and where I have preached. I find that particularly thrilling when I know the inexperience and nervousness of some of the group members leading the service.

It must be obvious that not everyone who attends the church wants the demanding involvement which housegroup membership entails. Most do, though—we have 150 members in housegroups at present and the number is constantly growing as new people are converted and added to the church. In addition to all the facilities a parish church normally provides for parishioners, we try to provide extra for those who don't, at present, want such a demanding involvement. So we have a weekly morning fellowship group and a weekly evening fellowship. These are not integrated into the main housegroup pattern with its responsibilities for the 'mini-parishes', its practical rotas and its housegroup service rota. These two groups are simply for teaching, prayer and fellowship. There is also the Commitment Group for new folk which over a period of a few months teaches the basics of the Christian life and the vision we have for the church.

On Sunday evenings we are developing a system of teaching course groups which run in parallel from 7.00 pm to 7.45 pm before Evening Praise begins at 8.00 pm. There is no assignment of people to these groups; they are open to anyone. So far we have established systematic courses on Christian Beliefs, Christian Family Life, Witnessing and Leadership. Soon we plan to add a course on The Defence of the Faith (Apologetics). Notes are produced for these courses and we invite members to do some homework between sessions.

It has worried some people that we have put our vision down on paper, and encouraged our members to understand and work actively towards its fulfilment—especially within the context of housegroups. They fear that this makes us seem exclusive. Others criticise and caricature what we are doing. I have thought and prayed long and hard over these points and carefully weighed up even the most inaccurate criticism. But the church is deeply involved in evangelism. Numbers are growing in the congregation and in the housegroups. 82.4% of the regular adult members of the congregation live within one mile of our two churches. They are, therefore, truly parish or local churches not eclectic congregations. Since there is a wide choice of churches within reach, it appears we are catering satisfactorily for some 250 *local* adults who regularly attend plus about 100 young people. Also it seems to me that every local church is to some degree eclectic. It is either too high, too low, too traditional, too modern, too lively, too unfriendly or too informal. No local church is everyone's cup of tea. Far from it. I believe that we are at least providing significantly more facilities for all our parishioners than the minimum requirement of a parish church and that we are no more eclectic than the average church.

We have always tried to provide a variety of worship in the parish. Until 1982 we had informal morning services in both churches using the ASB service as a framework. At St. Mary's there was a 4.30 p.m. traditional service from the old prayerbook on alternate Sundays. Then we had the spontaneous Evening Praise in both churches. On November 1st 1981, we combined for Evening Praise at St. Mary's—although the building wasn't really big enough. It was quite remarkable how through prophecies and other contributions we sensed the Lord was stressing the need for unity in the parish. This conviction had grown stronger by the time the elders spent a 24-hour retreat together in January 1982.

Back in 1979, we were expecting the arrival of our first senior curate. Before that we had had a deacon straight from college. The conviction had dawned on us that this more experienced man should have responsibility for one of the churches whilst I concentrated on the other. With my soft spot for St. Mary's, I anticipated that I would probably concentrate my attention there with the curate at Emmanuel. But as we prayed it became clear that I was to major on Emmanuel. The PCC voted unanimously in favour of this, but I found it difficult to delegate one of the churches, especially lovely old St. Mary's. Besides, the family and I felt at home at St. Mary's whereas we didn't at Emmanuel. But the Lord's will was clear, and for over two years I was an occasional visitor to St. Mary's.

But in January 1982 at our elders' retreat the Lord was stressing the need for the whole eldership to minister to the whole congregation (i.e. the people meeting in both churches). It was not until the summer that we sensed we knew how to achieve this. The curate was about to leave to become an incumbent elsewhere. We wanted to draw the whole congregation together and to provide a variety of services. In July, the PCC unanimously decided to move St. Mary's morning service to 9.30 am, making it fairly traditional. The 4.30 pm traditional service remained unaltered. This change had various advantages in our two-church parish. It gave maximum choice in worship—people could attend both traditional and informal services. The clergy and other elders could much more easily be involved in both churches. For example, I would often be both at St. Mary's 9.30 am and Emmanuel 10.30 am on the same morning. It also meant that the whole people of God could meet together, worship together and learn together at Emmanuel (the only building big enough) at a time which did not conflict with St. Mary's services. This bringing everyone together for regular fellowship and ministry was vital to our vision of unity and most of the St. Mary's people made the effort to join in the morning and/or evening worship at Emmanuel from November 1982.

Sadly, however, whilst all this was happening a potentially very divisive situation arose in the church. It concerned one of the old style housegroups. There were a few folk who were disenchanted with the church. A number of them were involved in this group. I then began to realise that other people with negative reactions were starting to opt out of other groups to join this one. The danger signals were clear. When I met with this group to discuss this and other problems, most of them threw all sorts of negative criticisms at me for most of the evening.

I was reluctant to exert my authority and close the group down. So I met them again and suggested that they discontinued as an official housegroup but that they

144

might wish to continue meeting for coffee and fellowship simply as friends. This seemed a more than reasonable compromise. I went on to ask them however, not to invite new people to the group. The danger was that these people would be rather negative. Unfortunately, this condition was not acceptable to them. After more fruitless discussions over the next six months eventually I was forced to ask them to close the group down. Sadly nearly all of them left the church. In spite of my reluctance to exert my authority and my willingness to compromise perhaps more than was wise, the incident ended negatively. I found all this very painful but felt that at least I had done my best to maintain unity in the church. Perhaps the Lord was pruning the church in order to strengthen it and to encourage growth.

13: Reaching Out

There are dangers in 'hearing' the Lord through inter-cession and prophecy. One is that, having genuinely 'heard', we then rush off and try to fulfil God's will in our own strength and wisdom. Another is that we sit back and say, 'Praise the Lord for what he's going to do. Now we can concentrate on something else whilst He gets on with it.' We could have done this over our outreach. For a number of years God had been saying we would be reaching out to other churches, not only to receive from them but to give encouragement to them. More recently God had called us to be concerned for the Jews and Israel. But we knew what this meant. Having 'heard' Him we had to get down to further intercession for two reasons. One was to discover what methods He wanted us to use to fulfil His will. The second was to pray His will into practical reality.

During 1982 a deep change was occurring in the congregation. For years I had taught and challenged about witnessing and mission. After all it was a duty that any self-respecting church would aim to do something about. But now outreach, local or further afield, was beginning to grip the church. Since then it has become the dominant factor in our interest, prayers, giving and activities. Yet for some seven years, this was not so, nor could it be worked up beyond a rather insignificant level. Then God's time arrived for it to happen and the Holy Spirit brought it about.

On one occasion that year a leader said to me, 'I

146

believe that next year it will be right for us to put on a special meeting to explain our vision to anyone in the area who is interested.' 'Do you think so?' I replied. My non-committal reply was covering up some rather negative thoughts. 'We can't do that,' I thought to myself. 'We're nothing special. The congregation isn't that big. Besides, its not really Anglican to put on such a meeting. We're supposed to work in our small corner and not make a song and dance about it. In any case, not many people would come.' I was not exactly full of faith! But I didn't want to let other people know that.

However, over the next few months the conviction began to grow in me that such a meeting would be right. We visited various well known churches of different denominations which were moving in renewal. We always went hoping to receive a lot. But we found ourselves coming away disappointed, not because the churches weren't good but because some of them didn't seem to be significantly further on than we were. Initially we couldn't understand this and thought perhaps we were being critical. Then gradually it dawned on us that God was saying, 'Yes, you are very ordinary people. Without Me you're nothing. But don't minimise what I am doing among you and don't limit what I want to do with you. I want you to encourage my people elsewhere.'

So it was that we planned a special Celebration for March 1983 entitled 'Charismatic Renewal in the End Times', advertised it widely to Essex churches, and prayed. On the night Emmanuel was packed with people from many different churches including a good contingent from the housechurches. During the praise and worship at the beginning I felt quite nervous. The Movement Team did an excellent presentation based on the Parable of the Ten Virgins. It vividly brought home the need to recognise the urgency of the Church's mission in the present age. I then spoke on the Restoration of

147

the Church to biblical principles such as those taught in Eph. 4:1–16 including unity in the truth, every member ministry, mature loving relationships etc. The talk was set in the context of the Signs of the End Times as taught in various New Testament passages.

As a follow-up to that meeting we organised regular Celebrations at 8.00 pm on the second Sunday of each month in Emmanuel. These have been fairly well attended by members of other churches.

In August 1983 a team of eleven of us led a week's houseparty at Ashburnham for another parish. This was the first time we had embarked on such an extensive project. I led two teaching sessions each day on 'Living the Christian life in the Last Days'. Bob Wilkinson and I shared four leaders seminars. Patricia led a daily seminar on Prophecy. Sue Wilkinson and Fiona Lindsay led seminars on Intercession. Pete and Jan Acton led workshops on the use of Movement, Drama and the Gifts of the Spirit in Worship. Some of our young church leaders held morning sessions for the children and teenagers.

We found the week a time of great blessing. The Holy Spirit clearly anointed the worship and teaching in the public sessions and seminars. Also the private counselling was quite amazing in terms of its depth and what God did through it. We saw people healed, delivered from demonic influences and transformed by the Lord. There was deep repentance and sacrificial obedience. Marriages and other relationships were healed and brought on to a right footing. Because of the large number wanting counselling, the team often worked into the early hours. But the benefits to the team were enormous. I watched them mature spiritually before my eyes as they entered into new depths of intercession. We experienced a very deep unity as a team.

Later in the year we decided that we should plan a

residential Church Leaders' Weekend in the parish. We put a small advertisement in a few Christian newspapers and magazines. In September 1984, 120 Christian leaders, including a good number of clergy and ministers, descended on Hawkwell from all over the country. Some came from as far afield as Lancashire and Tyneside. Those who came from any distance stayed in the homes of our churchmembers, for which we made a very modest charge to cover expenses. I led sessions on The Spiritual Qualifications of Leadership, Structuring the Church Charismatically, Unity in the Church, Evangelism, Spiritual Warfare and Prophetic Witness. It was a thrilling weekend with a deep sense of the Lord's presence. Even from the very first worship song we experienced the anointing of the Holy Spirit on the meetings.

In 1982 God had clearly convinced us that the main emphasis of our mission interest would be by direct link with other churches in this country and overseas. It would involve going as well as praying and giving. In all such links the whole church would be involved, not just me. For example, whenever possible I take a team of churchmembers with me. Some contribute publicly, others give prayer backing and perhaps help with ministry to individuals. This is a natural expression of our unity and commitment to one another. I would not think of going off to 'do my own thing' independently of the church.

However, we knew we were not to exclude links with missionary organisations. In the Autumn Patricia and I briefly visited the headquarters of Youth with a Mission (YWAM) in Sussex. We spent an afternoon with the British Director Lynn Green and with Barry Austin. Immediately we sensed a bond with them and a similarity of vision. In March 1983, Lynn and Barry visited Emmanuel and challenged us further about national and overseas outreach. YWAM works in over 40 countries combining evangelism, teaching and mercy ministries. They have a large ship, the 'Anastasis' (11,695 tons) which they use for famine relief and refugee work as well as for teaching and evangelistic purposes. They make extensive use of short-term workers as well as long-term.

Following the YWAM weekend one of our young women has joined the mission full time, working mainly in this country. We sent one young man to work in the YWAM outreach to the Olympic Games in Los Angeles. Several of our teenagers and adults have done work in the summer in London outreach. This short-term experience is invaluable for those who have been involved. We share with YWAM a very deep concern for London as our capital city.

We have similar links with Good News Crusade which is an evangelistic Mission working mainly in this country. Again, we are supporting one young couple from Hawkwell who are working full time with the Crusade and others have worked short term in the Summer. All of this fits in with our vision for our people to have direct involvement—long term or short term—in mission rather than only praying and giving. Needless to say, we benefit as a church from our members gaining this experience.

1983 also saw development of our interest in the Jewish people and Israel. In April we celebrated Yom Hashoai—Holocaust Remembrance Day. We remembered with sorrow and penitence not only the 6 million Jews slaughtered by Nazi Germany, but also the horrific persecution of the Jews down through the centuries by the so-called Christian Church. I wrote in Focus that day, 'Over the centuries many foul and bloody persecutions of the Jews have taken place in the name of the church. The Crusades of the 11th Century onwards were such, as were the many forced 'conversions' of Jews and repressive anti-Jewish legislation. Gentile Christians should appreciate that, not unnaturally, Jews tend to see Christianity in the light of the dreadful history of "Christian" anti-Semitism.'

We also prayed on that day against the resurgence of the Satanic spirit of anti-Semitism in Germany, France, Britain and America. And we remembered the many Jews being prevented from leaving Russia. Of course, the Lebanon war was in progress and Israel was being severely criticised. Sadly there are a growing number of what I call 'Israel nutters'—Christians who believe that Israel can do no wrong. These people bring into disrepute a genuine, God-given concern for Israel on the part of millions of Christians. However, from the research I did in those months, it became clear that all too often Israel was the victim of sophisticated Palestinian propaganda. I believe many highly publicised 'sins' of Israel in Lebanon were, in fact, false accusations. Nevertheless, Israel is a secular state, probably no more religious than this country. It has its political and religious extremists, some of whom are as bad as any PLO terrorist.

In June the local Orthodox Rabbi showed us round the synagogue. Afterwards I wrote to thank him and added:

'In the last year or so we sense God has drawn our attention to the Jewish people in general and Israel in particular. Our visit to you reminded us of our rich heritage in the Old Testament and our indebtedness to God's ancient people.

'As we look back in history we are appalled at the way in which so-called Christians have maltreated the Jews—whether verbally or physically. Furthermore, this country's treatment of the Jews before and after the setting up of Israel—and even more recently—has sometimes been

seriously unjust. This together with modern anti-semitism
makes us feel very ashamed.

  'However, we are thrilled at the amazing way God
has preserved the state of Israel and at the remarkable
achievements in that Land. It figures very prominently in
our prayers . . .'.

We were pleased to hear later that this letter was
pinned up on the synagogue noticeboard and remained
there for months. A year later we were glad to help the
local Jewish community in a practical way. They were
holding an exhibition of Jewish life in Southend Library
and needed help with stewarding. Quite a number of
our church members spent many hours looking after this
exhibition.

  In Holy Week 1983, Bob and Sue Wilkinson, Patricia
and I had met for an evening of prayer about the church.
What happened was a total surprise. Half-way through
the evening Patricia and I both had a deep conviction
that we needed to lay down the work in Hawkwell. We
were to give it back to God. It was a very profound
experience because we realised it meant that God might
take us away from Hawkwell. This must have been the
Holy Spirit because nothing could have been further
from our thinking before that evening. Suddenly, we felt
different. Instead of being totally absorbed by the
church, as we had been for eight years, we felt at a
distance from it. The feelings were quite disturbing but
we believed they were in God's will for us. What it would
lead to we did not know.

  About a fortnight later we had a brief meeting at our
request with the Home Director of the Church's Ministry
amongst the Jews (C.M.J.), Derek Ryder. The reason
we had asked to meet him was to find out about the
Anglican work in Israel because of our interest as a
church. We were not at all thinking of our personal

future in ministry. What we heard about C.M.J. impressed us but one casual remark by Derek made us prick up our ears. He mentioned that they were looking for a new Field Director for the work in Israel. Our reaction was contradictory. On the one hand it seemed ludicrous, even presumptuous to think it had any relevance to us. On the other hand it fascinated us. However, we soon afterwards dismissed the idea and forgot about it.

A few weeks later Bob and Sue Wilkinson took the initiative, after sharing it with us, of asking the PCC to send us to Israel on a pilgrimage and fact finding trip for the church. They unanimously agreed to do this. At the same time, a friend of ours had told us about an American couple, Alfred and Memory Sawyer, who were about to go out to Jerusalem, where Alfred was to become vicar of Christ Church, Jerusalem. We were interested to meet them from the point of view of possibly maintaining contact with them.

So in early Summer we visited Alfred and Memory in Finchley. Immediately we sensed a bond between us as we chatted about Israel and the church. Then they mentioned the Field Director's job again. We had not thought about it for some months, but our chat with them awakened our interest and we were convinced that we must at least explore the possibility. Shortly afterwards we had a long informal discussion with the General Director of C.M.J. Following this, we realised that we needed others to pray with us in addition to Bob and Sue. So we shared it in confidence with about a dozen of the leaders. After prayer they were convinced we should explore the C.M.J. job more. So we made formal application. Meanwhile, Alfred preached at Emmanuel and he and Memory immediately endeared themselves to the congregation.

At the beginning of September, we began our trip

to Israel. As we flew over Europe many thoughts and questions were going through my mind. This was truly the journey of a lifetime. Ever since I could remember, I had known about the Holy Land and had formed mental pictures of it. What would it really be like? Would it be disappointing? What if I didn't like it? Were we going to live there? What would it be like as a place to live? There was the war situation and the terrorism. And the heat! I'm not exactly a hot-house plant. Patricia and I have often laughed about an incident on our honeymoon. In the narrow streets of Mousehole in Cornwall, I walked up the shady side whilst she walked in the sun. That was only a bit of fun. But the heat in the Middle East was a different matter. What would it be like to work in it? Our teenage children, Rachel and Michel, were with us on the trip. How would they take to life in Israel? However, the excitement of the trip counterbalanced these concerns as we flew out over the Mediterranean.

The plane was beginning to descend in the darkness. We peered out of the window and suddenly we saw the lights of Tel Aviv below us. At last, our first glimpse of Israel! We were flying by British Airways and many people around us were British. No one else seemed to be planning to fulfil tradition, so we did it. Quietly, as a family, we sang 'Hevenu Shalom aleichem' ('We bring you peace') as we touched down. It was mid evening and the temperature was still 84°F. The heat hit us as we left the plane. Soon we were on our way to Jerusalem and the driver took us up the Mount of Olives. There below us we could just make out the old city with the Dome of the Rock standing out defiantly on Temple Mount.

In the early hours I was woken up by the sound of the call from the minarets dotted around East Jerusalem. It seemed an eerie but fascinating sound with a strange attraction. Spiritually it was alien, proclaiming in effect a denial of Jesus as Son of God. It was Sunday and after breakfast we attended a service at the Garden Tomb. Whether or not it is the actual tomb (and the evidence is remarkable) this was a most moving experience. How important the empty cross and the empty tomb are to our Faith! After the service, we walked through the old city, itself a step back over centuries, to Christ Church for the end of their morning service.

The week in Jerusalem passed so quickly. I spent one afternoon on my own meditating at the foot of Skull Hill—a profound spiritual experience. Our hotel was only a few hundred yards from the hill. More than once that week I went up on the roof at the end of the after-noon and sat alone. At sunset Jerusalem looks very beautiful. The stone begins to glow with a soft pink colour. From where I sat I could see the top of Skull Hill where, perhaps, the great sacrifice took place. Beyond it was the old city, and further away still, the Wilderness of Judaea. I shall never forget those experiences. Neither shall I forget the ancient Roman Pavement beneath the Ecce Homo Convent. On those very stones Jesus was tortured. Nor will I forget the remains of Caiaphas' house or the ancient steps from the Kidron Valley up which Jesus climbed after his arrest.

The whole week was a kaleidoscope of fascinating and moving experiences: the neat Christian Arab town of Bethlehem; the heat of the desert around Beersheba; the politically volatile situation in Hebron; Ashkelon and the sinister revival of Dagon Worship; the Valley of Elah where David killed Goliath. In our spare time we managed to speak to the previous Field Director of C.M.J., finding out more about the job which was by now interesting us so deeply. We also discussed the situation in Israel with the International Christian Embassy and with the Sisters of Mary who live on the Mount of Olives.

On the Saturday we travelled up to Tiberias via Megiddo, Nazareth and Nain. Then in the late afternoon sun we caught our first glimpse of the beautiful Sea of Galilee—misty blue in the valley beneath us, 700 feet below sea level. The Sunday morning communion in the YMCA Chapel overlooking the Sea of Galilee and its surrounding hills was a most moving experience. I was surprised that a trip across the Sea was so meaningful. Later we travelled across the battle-scarred Golan Heights to the foot of majestic Mount Hermon, towering 9000 feet above the borders of Israel, Lebanon and Syria. From there we returned to Tiberias via Caesarea Philippi, one of the sources of the River Jordan. The ancient rock face there gave special significance to the statement Jesus made there to Peter that on the rock of his confession he would build his church.

We returned to Tel Aviv and the children returned to England with the rest of the pilgrimage party on the Thursday. Patricia and I stayed on to visit the C.M.J. centres. We greatly enjoyed our stay at Emmanuel House, Jaffa. It was good to meet the expatriate workers as well as Israelis there. Towards the end of our stay we spent a few days at Stella Carmel on the top of Mount Carmel. This has rightly been called the Alpine scenery of Israel. Near there we looked out over the vast plain of Armageddon. We could so easily see its significance as a place of past and future battles.

During our three weeks in Israel, both whilst on the organised pilgrimage and whilst on our own, we made a point of visiting the homes of some Jewish believers in various parts of the country. One afternoon we talked to an Israeli who had come to faith in Christ a few years earlier. He was active in the local group of believers. He described the activities of the small minority of Jewish extremists who persecuted them. Stones had been thrown at their windows when the house was packed with people for a fellowship meeting. Their car tyres had been slashed. One morning they went out and discovered posters all over their town describing them by name as enemies of Israel. As I listened to all this and sat in the very place where it was happening, I was profoundly moved. One thing he said brought tears to my eyes. 'You know, Tony, the believers in Russia have a far worse time than we do.' I felt thoroughly ashamed of the way my few experiences of being falsely accused had sometimes rather got me down. Another Jewish believer friend was accused of keeping a brothel in which young Israelis were induced to convert to Christianity. Sometimes these accusations have been published nationally. I must make it clear this persecution is the work of a tiny fringe of extremists.

I found Israel lived up to my expectations as far as pilgrimage was concerned. And modern Israel is a miracle of survival and growth. But we were looking at the country from the point of view of living there. One afternoon Patricia and I were on a beach right up on the Lebanon border. It was hot and sticky and the place was, like many places in Israel, covered with litter. Also we had found that Israelis tend to be rather aggressive in their life style. Probably all that they've been through encourages this. We had sensed very heavy spiritual oppression, not least over Jerusalem. For the second time during our trip I shared with Patricia that although I was ready to obey the Lord if He wanted us in Israel, I certainly didn't want to live there. After this, we met up with Alfred and Memory Sawyer in Jaffa. After discussing and praying with them about the opportunities for ministry in Israel, I felt much more positive. My dislike of certain aspects of life in Israel came more into perspective.

So we returned to England and shortly afterwards the interviews took place for the Field Director's job in

Jerusalem. We spent 24 hours at a conference centre during which we had several very searching interviews. By this time we were all but convinced that God was going to take us out to Israel. We had faced the emotional aspects of leaving Hawkwell. In fact, I felt remote from the church and found it difficult to want to be involved. Our hearts were in Jerusalem in spite of the unattractive aspects of Israel. During the selection conference, we were both praying very much that God would stop us if we were not the right people. But, having worked out a long list of pros and cons, it seemed highly likely, both to us and to the leaders in the parish, that the job was right.

A day or so later a letter from C.M.J. came through the post. It said that, although they couldn't give any clear reason, they felt that we were not the right ones for the job. It had been a very close thing but they had chosen the other couple. We were bitterly disappointed. It seemed meaningless. What reason could there be for this to happen? We felt remote from the church. The leaders had begun to plan for our departure and to become accustomed to the emotional impact of that. We had been prepared to overcome our natural desire to stay in England and in Hawkwell and our aversion to aspects of Israel. Now this. Why?

With the benefit of hindsight, I think I can now answer that question. I believe God wanted us to be willing to offer Hawkwell back to Him rather like Abraham was called upon to offer Isaac. The Lord has done a lot in Hawkwell and we had been totally absorbed in the parish for almost nine years. The work could so easily become an idol. It could become more important than obedience to God. And so the Lord had to test whether He came first or His work did.

But we believe that the Lord was not playing games with us about Israel. We made many contacts over there

158

and we are quite convinced that some of these contacts will develop to become long term opportunities of mutual learning and encouragement. It is over two years since the Lord gave us a definite call to be concerned for Israel and we have a tremendous concern for the welfare and witness of the church there. We are now just beginning to glimpse the possibilities of this concern being practically expressed. We sense it is God's time for action.

On the other hand, although we have had a deep concern for the church in the Communist world, we do not sense that the Lord has yet shown us the exact form our involvement should take. On our journey to Israel we flew over Albania. Far below us we could see something of that remote country which claims to be the world's first totally atheist state. Officially there is no church there at all. Patricia and I found it a moving experience to be looking down on a land which is in such spiritual darkness. Similarly, for all our concern, we don't yet feel we know God's will for our involvement with the Third World in its poverty, other than to give sacrificially. God has his timing. We are sometimes a little impatient but we have learned to wait until we sense He is telling us to act.

Meanwhile, evangelism in the parish continued to develop. In 1983 we began a new venture called the Faith Sharing Group. We realise that many people in this country now have no church background. They often do not understand what goes on in church nor see its relevance. In fact, many people would feel 'out of it' if they came. Some are actually afraid to come because they don't know what to expect. Yet there is a great spiritual hunger amongst the population of Britain. Sadly this all too often leads people into astrology, the occult or the wierd cults. We sensed the need for a 'half-way house' between the parish and the church. This is where the Faith Sharing Group came in.

What happens is this. A married couple open their home and invite neighbours and contacts to come for coffee and a chat about the Faith. It is very informal, normally beginning with coffee and general social chat. Then very sensitively the leader, who is experienced and trained in witnessing, broaches the subject of the Faith, unless it has come up spontaneously. From then on the leader guides the discussion, answers questions etc. There is no pressure and no obligation. The group will meet for a few sessions with the same people, in fact, as long as it seems relevant.

We have found the Faith Sharing Groups (there are now two) are perhaps the most exciting aspect of our recent evangelism. So many people have come to real faith in Christ through them. Of the first 50 people to attend, 20 made a commitment to Christ and a further six, who were already believers, received help to overcome doubts and problems.

Sometimes people who have attended the Faith Sharing Group finally make a commitment to Christ in a Guest Service. At other times, a person attends the church, perhaps at a Guest Service first and then goes to the group where he eventually commits his life to Christ. The group leaders do, of course, provide private help for those requesting it. When someone who has not attended the group makes a profession of faith in Christ at a service, we often invite them to the Faith Sharing Group where immediate follow up, clarification and consolidation of their decision can be achieved. After that, they are invited into the Commitment Group for longer term follow up.

In April 1984 we decided to purchase a page in a local free newspaper delivered to every house in the district. The layout editor was most helpful. In fact, he was quite enthused by this unusual project. We planned a page of testimonies with photographs and headings so that it

160

looked like a normal newspage. The testimonies were about conversion, physical healing and inner healing. The end result looked very attractive. We had phone calls from Christians in other churches saying how the page had helped them talk about the Gospel to relatives and friends.

At the same time we began a new venture which continued throughout the Summer within the parish. We had often used joyful praise, testimony, drama and movement in the church services. But the Creative Worship Team had, after prayer, come to the conclusion that they should take these activities out into the streets. They chose sites at each end of the parish adjacent to shopping centres. Looking back, I think one of the most helpful aspects was the joyful praise. We ran a public address system and an electric piano off a car battery and quite a large group sang joyful songs, expressing their happiness in a way which communicated to passers by. Other churchmembers distributed leaflets and got into conversation with anyone willing to chat. I felt the simple message that these people from the local parish church actually thoroughly enjoyed praising God was very worthwhile. However, brief testimonies, comments, dramas and movements were also used. People did start coming to church as a result and we keep finding people who, although they are not yet coming to church, were really impressed with the team's presentation. The team has also done a similar presentation at a school fete.

During Spring 1984 there had been a television series 'Jesus: the Evidence' attacking the Christian Faith. We circulated to every home in the parish a leaflet which corrected this series. We believe that one evidence for the living Jesus is what he does through prayer in the lives of ordinary people today. We included with this leaflet the story of one or two people who had recently committed their lives to Christ. But we also included the

161

story of the healing of a two year old boy. Andrew was born with a condition called Hypospadias which requires an operation. Just before Easter the doctor said that the need for an operation had become urgent. Andrew was prayed for at the Easter Guest Service. I remember he was not very happy about it and yelled a good deal whilst his father held him. However, four days after he was prayed for he saw the specialist who said: 'There isn't anything wrong here . . . certainly an operation is out of the question.'

More recently we believe God has begun to give us a vision of offering a tithe of the parish to God. In other words, we are aiming at one tenth of the 10,000 parishioners coming to know Christ. We are not regarding this as an ultimate aim because we would always seek to win more people. But it is a definite aim and we are beginning to plan towards it. At present we have a congregation of some 350 including 90 children under 16: so we are not a large church and we are ordinary people. What God has done here He could do anywhere.

We have been strong on Proclamation Evangelism i.e. situations where the Gospel is specifically proclaimed through sermons, conversations or literature. But we feel strongly now that we need to increase our Presence Evangelism. That is, we need to permeate local society showing the love of Christ. That will mean more involvement in local affairs, organisations and events. It will also mean strengthening the caring aspect of our outreach.

We are aware, however, that people are primarily won through intercession. Such prayer releases the power of God. Our ultimate concern is for a great Revival of the Faith brought about by the sovereign work of the Holy Spirit. We long to see thousands come to repentance and faith in our Nation, even without any human agency or evangelism. It is my conviction that God wants to do this and that it is the only real answer to the country's spiritual needs. Only then will the approximately 90% who don't go to church be won for Christ. But history shows that the condition of revival is that Christians should put their lives right with God as far as they know how, and become involved in extensive prayer and fasting.

14: Prayer Battle Against Principalities and Powers

'It may just be a one-off problem in the lives of a few people. On the other hand you might find that when you've dealt with it in one person it seems to fasten on someone else and so on. Then it may well be that there is a concerted spiritual attack on you. For example it may be a Satanist group praying against you.' The speaker was a minister friend of mine in Devon. I was down in Exmouth to lead the holiday Bible Week at Haldon Court in June 1979. This man had previously been a great help to me and so I had sought him out to discuss some pressing church problems with him. I couldn't understand why a number of people seemed to be gripped with a very negative, even vitriolic attitude of rebellious criticism. For a long time I'd just put it down to human nature and the conservative reaction to change in the church. But in spite of my scepticism about the presence of demonic activity even I had to conclude eventually that there was something more than human nature here.

By Summer 1979 I'd just about reached the point where I could believe in the possibility of one or two people in the church being demonically oppressed by a spirit of rebellious criticism. But I wasn't really ready to cope with the idea of some heavier, concerted spiritual attack on the church, especially if it included Satanists praying against us. So I filed away in my mind the remark my friend had made. I hoped it was not true of Hawkwell but I didn't forget it.

In early 1981 I began to realise that another problem area in the parish stemmed from other than human origin. Before that time I don't think I would ever have thought this could happen. Over the years we had had various good men as treasurers. They were committed, hard working, capable and honest. Some of them had professional accountancy qualifications. But there were always problems. The giving was adequate but the treasurers seemed under tremendous pressure. Some became ill. In spite of the treasurers' competence and dedication the accounts sometimes seemed to be muddled or inefficient. I should add that this was always eventually sorted out and there was not even a suggestion of any dishonesty. But we couldn't understand it. Problems seemed to dog the treasurers. One treasurer's wife said of her husband, 'I can't understand it. Whenever he's been working on the books, its not just tiredness, there's something else wrong.'

It became painfully obvious that we needed to pray about this matter and ask the Lord for wisdom. As we did this we began to understand. I have already said that the Christian Church's attitude to money can sometimes be quite wrong. There can be selfishness, uncharitable arguments and bitter divisions over money. We began to sense that this had happened in the past in Hawkwell. We don't know when or who was involved. We don't need to. But this had been so bad that it had given an opportunity for a demonic oppression to affect the parish accounts and treasurers.

So in the PCC meeting in May 1981, we brought all the account books out and placed them on the table. I prayed authoritatively cutting off this influence and asking God to anoint the treasurer with a new freedom. There was a remarkable change. Since then the accounting has been so smooth that it required quite an adjustment to relate to such efficiency!

This incident started me thinking about another aspect of the Church. By and large our Young Church Groups had been going quite well except for the junior section. Again I am not questioning the competence and dedication of the leaders. But there seemed to have been problem after problem with this group. These were not just the usual ups and downs of a Christian Education group. There seemed to be something 'heavy' about the department. Some of the leaders seemed to run into fairly serious spiritual problems. 'But just because you've discerned this oppression over the accounts, there's no need to go overboard and put all the parish problems down to the same thing,' I said to myself. 'After all, its possible to become fearful and even rather superstitious about supposed demonic influence.'

Then I remembered a quite remarkable experience I'd had several years before. For the first time I saw a new significance in it related to the Young Church. One evening, early in Spring 1975, we had a meeting of Young Church leaders (mostly from the junior section) to plan a children's holiday club. In the meeting I felt distant and uninvolved. It was as if I wasn't really there or part of the discussion. I put it down to the after effects of the tooth extraction I'd had in the afternoon. The next morning I stopped off at St. Mary's to have a time of prayer. I sat there gazing at the pages of the Bible but unable to concentrate or to pray properly. I was about to give up when the words 'Resist the devil' came into my mind. I dismissed the thought and tried to read the Bible still with no success. Again, but more forcefully, the words returned 'Resist the Devil'. I stopped and spoke out loud in the empty church, enthusiastically resisting Satan. Immediately I felt a tremendous release and lightness of spirit. I was so full of joy and praise, I

166

had to calm myself down a bit before returning home for an interview.

Now, six years later, I began to see a new significance. It had been a Young Church meeting in which I had begun to experience such deep oppression. As with the accounts there was a long term oppression over the junior section of the Young Church. Since dealing with that in prayer the junior department has seemed to go well and smoothly, often more so than the infant and teenage groups. Certainly the old problems have gone.

I began to understand that the Devil could have a hold over a particular aspect of church life. And this could last for years, even over generations, unless it was dealt with through spiritual warfare. This wasn't just theory. On two occasions what was effectively prayer for deliverance had led to a remarkable release from long term and quite serious problems.

At the end of November 1981 Patricia had an experience which led us to understand more of the Devil's strategy against us. This is how she shared it with the Church:

'I want to share with you a very strange experience which I had last week. I believe that the spirit of criticism temporarily afflicted me.

'I have had a very painful ulcerating mouth for ten days or so, making me feel low generally. A combination of prayer and TCP(!) didn't seem to be having any effect and possibly a little resentment crept into my heart. This was the chance the enemy had been waiting for and he seized the opportunity to try to make *me* critical.

'I think you all know that normally I am very enthusiastic about everything that goes on in the church. When I go to meetings I look forward to them, longing for an opportunity to worship the Lord—excited about what He might do. But on Thursday at the Leaders' Fellowship, I felt like an outsider looking on. People all around me seemed "lost in wonder, love and praise", but I could not get involved and what's more, didn't want to. I felt that those who were leading had nothing to offer me and I did not want to contribute in any way.

'I put it all down to the ulcerating mouth. On Friday I again felt so low that Tony thought he had better pray with me. He sensed it was more than a physical problem and asked for wisdom.

'As he prayed quietly I found I was thinking about the church and to my surprise my attitude was very critical in a way that it had never been before.

'I felt like an onlooker, detached, even somewhat superior. I regarded everything that was going on in the church as rather pathetic. I began to think of those whom I know to be critical and sensed a fellow-feeling with them and a desire to discuss it all with them. Although it was all rather unpleasant and totally unlike me, I felt very hard with no wish to change.

'It was a bit like the experience of Adam and Eve, when they had taken the fruit. As they ate it their eyes were opened so that instead of seeing themselves and the world from God's point of view, they saw it all from a human and sinful angle. It was as if I had begun to taste of the fruit of criticism and was seeing the church from the point of view of human wisdom, not God's.

'It was only as Tony continued praying that I realised I was being afflicted by this demonic spirit which has entered our church — the spirit of criticism. It had taken advantage of me in a moment of weakness. Even then because of the power of the thing I had to make a conscious and deliberate act of will to renounce the desire to wallow in such feelings, because, unpleasant though they were, there was an attraction about them.

'As soon as I told God that I was willing to put such thoughts behind me, Tony was able to pray against the spirit and I was immediately back to my normal self.

168

'The ulcers remained, which showed they were not the cause of the experience, but I was able to praise God for allowing them.

'Eventually I was able to understand why God had permitted the temporary oppression. I now know how to pray for those who are critical of the church or have been influenced by the negative attitudes of others or by this spirit. I now know how destructive it is to be critical, how it affects a person's spiritual life and renders him completely unusable in what God is doing in the church.'

It was, however, a year later before we began to understand the extent of the spirit of rebellious criticism in the parish. A major aspect of its influence was rebellion. This influence had encouraged bitterly, critical rebellion, beyond what was humanly explicable, in various people. We have since learnt a good deal more about this subject. The main destructive influence in Hawkwell had been in the form of rebellion which is why it had been an important priority for us to get the matter of authority and submission into something like a correct balance. We have, however, come across churches elsewhere facing a very different destructive influence. For example, we know of churches riddled with adultery and immorality. Almost everywhere one looks one finds immoral relationships. I can say with reasonable confidence that immorality has been a very minor problem in Hawkwell Church. We have had to battle rather with destructive rebellion.

In Holy Week 1983 the elders sensed, after much prayer, that God had given us the go-ahead to bind this rebellious spirit. We had begun to learn that some demonic spirits were very powerful beings. I believe it is very important that Christians are very careful in dealing with these more powerful beings. We need to know through intercession that God has given us the go-ahead and the authority to bind them. It is God's initiative to bind them not ours. Matthew 18:18 literally reads, 'Whatever you bind on earth *shall have been* bound in heaven.' In other words, we can only bind what we sense God has bound already in heaven. We need to be sensitive to the prompting of the Holy Spirit. So we must be careful, though not fearful.

On the Good Friday evening we travelled around the parish proclaiming God's rule and victory over it. Since then there has been a dramatic absence of that old spirit of rebellion. The root of pernicious bitterly critical rebellion has been removed. We realised at the time that we had won a battle. But the war continues on other fronts.

Back in January 1982 we realised that St. Mary's needed to be liberated from some darker aspects of its long history. In spite of my soft spot for St. Mary's and my determination to develop it as a sister church to Emmanuel, the work never really got off the ground. True the curate fostered a happy fellowship but, generally speaking, leadership was not forthcoming. The young people's work never really developed. Yet a great deal of prayer and effort was put into the work there by various people. Always we seemed to hit a 'ceiling' beyond which we could not develop. I remember reacting negatively when a leader of many years standing in the parish had said, 'St. Mary's really died eight years ago.' He was referring to before my time. I didn't want to believe him, but I think he was unwittingly pointing to the spiritual oppression over the church.

The elders spent an evening of prayer about St. Mary's at the beginning of February. We began to sense in prayer that some root of bitterness had been sown many years ago in the church. Also we were concerned at any paganism which had affected the church or the site over the centuries—before or since the church's foundation 900 years ago. In the middle of February the elders spent a day of prayer and fasting in St. Mary's. It seemed a

170

good time but, looking back, I cannot see that a great deal changed in the situation. Maybe we lacked experience and understanding. Maybe we mistook the Lord's timing. It is perhaps more likely that we should have persisted in prayer beyond that day. It is, of course, important that two years later we began to understand more about the demonic opposition we were confronting. Meanwhile we wanted to be careful because we were 'feeling our way'. However, we probably delayed unnecessarily before finally dealing with the situation more adequately in early 1984.

By that time we had begun to sense in prayer other 'darker' things which had happened in the long history of St. Mary's, and we felt it was high time to act. This conviction was born out of prayer by the leadership and the prayer cells, all of whom reported back to the elders. Bob Wilkinson and I had been on a 24 hour retreat at the beginning of February and we felt the Lord was urging us to take action.

So on Monday evening, February 13th, two years to the day since the elders' first day of prayer for St. Mary's, all the leaders met in Emmanuel Hall for prayer. After an hour of intercession Bob and I with the four leaders of housegroups near St. Mary's went down to the church, leaving the leaders praying up at Emmanuel. For the next two hours the six of us prayed in St. Mary's, cutting it off from anything wrong in its past. I took the lead. The others contributed what they felt was important. We prayed about the ministry of all the rectors, going through the list by name, and we prayed throughout the building at key points, thinking of any way God's name may have been dishonoured there over the centuries, for example, people taking communion in an unworthy manner. By the end of the time we felt satisfied that the job had been done thoroughly. Then at 11.00 pm we went out to pray in the churchyard pausing at various

171

points. Fortunately the driver of the police car which passed did not see this strange group of men gathering around a grave in the moonlight!

From that time onwards, people testified to a new spiritual atmosphere in St. Mary's. We are not without problems there. But at least they are modern problems and not results of any darker aspects of the church's history. Whilst the work at Emmanuel goes ahead in leaps and bounds, we are still feeling our way towards a breakthrough at St. Mary's.

During 1984, a group of men have met in the early morning each week to pray for the parish. Part of the time they have walked the streets praying for the residents and asking God to guide their prayers. And God has guided them. Sometimes in my absence, they have discerned in prayer something about a particular home they have passed. On more than one occasion when they have reported back to me, I have actually known the situation in the home through normal human contact and realised the group's discernment was accurate. Gradually over the months they have covered the whole parish. We see this as part of 'possessing the land' for the Lord and proclaiming his Lordship over it. Any rule which the powers of darkness have over the parish is usurped from God. By rights it belongs to Him and we want to see his rule established in it.

15: Prophetic Witness

'I'm only called to be responsible for this parish, thank God,' wrote a fellow incumbent in a letter to me recently, 'And that's quite enough for me!' I felt a deep sadness at this remark. How was it possible to maintain such a short-sighted, parochial attitude when very serious errors were being tolerated in the Church of England? Then I remembered that for most of my ministry this had largely been my attitude. I had known there was a lot wrong with the Church of England but that was nothing to do with me. When some of my Free Church friends asked how I could be part of a church which tolerated seriously unbiblical views on theology and morality, I had a stock answer: the law of the church stated scripture is the supreme authority and the local Anglican Church is free to fulfil its mission. It wasn't my fault if some clergy denied the supremacy of scripture or weren't doing a very good job in their parishes. Besides, we were always told at college, 'If you find the perfect church, don't join it, you'll spoil it.'

However, my contacts with the housechurch movement up to Spring 1982 had caused me to think more deeply about this issue. Was I not guilty by association if I was silent about the serious faults in the Church of England? These errors tended to get publicity and the general public would think they were the normal views of the clergy—including me. Furthermore, the clever little statement about finding the perfect church was no excuse for not trying to have as pure a church as possible.

The New Testament certainly called for such purity. Jesus said, 'Be perfect as your Father in heaven is perfect'. It was quite wrong for me to react cynically to his command.

By the summer of 1982, some three months after the Ministers' Conference at the Housechurch headquarters in Bradford, I knew the Lord was not calling us to leave the Church of England for the housechurches. I wrote in Focus about the problems in the Anglican Church and asked, 'Should we get out then and join a better denomination? No I don't believe we should. All the other main denominations seem just about as bad . . . At present and perhaps for years to come the Lord is calling us to stay put and to witness both to His truth and to His judgment . . . we must take action and speak out prophetically God's Word to the wider church.' Looking back on that statement, I think all I was really sure about was that we were not to join the housechurches or another denomination. I had not finally rejected the idea that God might be calling us to leave the Anglican Church and just go independent. Besides in those days any prophetic speaking out to the wider church seemed very remote if not ludicrous.

A year later doubts about the rightness of remaining in the Church of England returned, but for a very different reason. Would it not be better to be free of the burden of buildings (especially ancient ones), diocesan quotas and the restrictions of tradition, parish boundaries and the like? We'd be able to concentrate on the real task of the church. One day in Autumn 1983 Patricia and I went for a walk in the woods near Hawkwell. As we trudged through the fallen leaves in the bright morning sunlight we talked and prayed about this issue. By the time we returned to the car, I was beginning to feel enthusiastic about the prospect. On the way back we had a look at a modern public hall which would be very adequate for

174

a Sunday morning service. Just think, the only overheads would be the weekly rental—no historic buildings, faculties and PCC discussions on fabric. Nearby were some small, modern houses. Compare that with our eleven rooms, 25 windows and 2½ acres. I realised as never before just how much time, money and energy we spend on buildings. As I contemplated leaving it all behind I felt a great weight lift off my mind. After all, the task of evangelising England was too urgent for us to be bogged down with such matters. In fact, if we let them hinder the task of evangelism, surely we'd have to answer to God for it.

We discussed the matter with some of the leaders and I chatted with the treasurer about the financial aspect. We were all confident that if we made the move, virtually the whole church would decide to join us. In our prayers we were concerned about what that would mean for the Parish Church of Hawkwell. We would certainly hope to maintain good relationships with the new incumbent. The prospect of dividing the local church distressed us but we felt it would be justified because of the urgent need to obey the Lord especially in evangelism. We had virtually reached the point of deciding to leave the Church of England.

Having reached that point, we spent a good deal of time in prayer and the more we prayed, the more uncertain we became that we should leave. On Friday February 3rd 1984, Bob Wilkinson and I attended a day conference held by John Noble and his team from the Romford strand of the Housechurch Movement at Pilgrim's Hall, Brentwood. The leader of the Community at Pilgrim's Hall, a personal friend of mine, had fairly recently left the Anglican Ministry over the issue of Baptism. Bob and I had arranged to stay on at the Hall for a 24 hour private retreat to come to a final decision about the future. It was in that perhaps rather unlikely context that I sensed a very definite call to stay in the Church of England. I experienced a deep awareness of the Lord's grief over the failings of the church and particularly over its ineffectiveness in winning the nation for Christ. But I also saw how the Church of England had a unique opportunity to influence the nation. All the contacts and means of communication at every level of national life were there, just waiting to be used. If only the church were radical in its obedience to Scripture in the Power of the Holy Spirit, it could quickly have a profound effect on the nation. I sensed the Lord hadn't given us up yet. He wanted to use us if only we'd put our house in order. Of course He could use other means in His power and maybe in the end He will have to do so. But He still hopes to use us although I don't know how long He'll wait for us.

During that retreat a deep concern was born in me for us Anglicans to put our house in order; to correct the unbiblical theology and morality; to submit to the authority of Scripture; to build the church in radical obedience to Scripture; and to proclaim the Gospel in the power and demonstration of the Holy Spirit. Interestingly, it was also during the retreat that, completely unexpectedly, the letter arrived from the publishers inviting me to write this book. Patricia rang me with the news so that we could pray about it on the retreat. We saw this as a confirmation of the rightness of staying in the Church of England. We also saw it as an opportunity to contribute towards the major task of calling the church to renew its life and mission in obedience to Scripture by the power of the Holy Spirit. I felt strongly that the Lord had called us to stay put but not to stay quiet. Otherwise we would, through our silence, be guilty by association of the serious errors tolerated by our national church. Little did I know what the Lord had on His agenda for us in the next few months. Our experience

176

of coming almost to the point of deciding to leave the Anglican Church was important. Just as we had had to offer our future in Hawkwell to the Lord in order to consider moving to Israel, so now, we had to put on the altar our future in the Church of England. It belonged to Him and He could take it away if He wished. The experience had helped us face up to the seriousness of the situation in the church and to the crisis of conscience which we sense an increasing number of Anglicans will have to face.

I had come home for coffee one morning to find Patricia rather upset. She had been reading the newspaper. A clergyman well known for his involvement with the Gay Christian Movement had been appointed to a position of honour in the church. Although the appointment had not been intended to draw attention to or support his views on homosexual practices, inevitably the press had taken it that way. As I read the article I knew this was it. I had got to burn my bridges and speak out about this. The prospect of coming into confrontation with a fellow clergyman and with the bishop concerned was quite painful. It goes very much against the grain to me as a person and as an Anglican. But I had no option. I had little hope of the decision being reversed but I just had to obey the Lord and raise a voice of protest. I would be the first to want to show the love of Christ to someone facing homosexual temptations and I have been privileged to help clergy facing them. But I am convinced that scripture condemns homosexual practices in very strong terms.

I conveyed my disapproval to the bishop concerned and eventually my stand gained publicity locally. One morning I was in the study expecting a churchmember to arrive for an appointment with Patricia and me. The phone rang and the editor of a local paper was on the line. He pointed out that they had discovered the clergyman in question was very seriously ill and the paper was hesitant about the story. I felt dreadful. I'd felt bad enough taking the action in the first place. I shall never forget sitting there after the phone call gazing through the study window for an hour or more. Patricia had to deal with the churchmember on her own. She said afterwards that I looked shocked and ill. 'What have I done?' I thought. 'Is it all a horrible mistake?' I began to pray, 'Lord, have I mistaken your call? Have I stepped out of your will? Will it be disastrously counter-productive? Shall I try and stop the whole protest?' Eventually, still feeling awful, I decided that in all conscience I could not back down. Later I learnt that the man in question was not as seriously ill as the news-paper editor had thought. I also discovered that his published views on homosexual practices and similar issues were far more serious than I had realised. Over the following few weeks I received much hard evidence that confirmed the rightness of my stand. Looking back I felt the Lord had allowed the whole incident as my 'baptism of fire' concerning taking public action on serious errors in the church. I was not anticipating what I was being prepared for.

Meanwhile we had been taking great interest in the national debate about Video Nasties and Children. We knew Dr. Clifford Hill who was organising the research and we knew the very heavy opposition from those with vested interests in the video industry. We decided that we would do our own survey, feeling that, being local, this would have more impact on parents and teachers in our area. With the co-operation of two schools we used a professionally prepared questionnaire with 990 local children. The results not only tallied with the general results of the national report, but they tallied with the figures in that report for a commuter area in the S.E. of England. We circulated our local finding to every home in the parish, and to over a hundred schools in the area. The local radio station and the press gave quite extensive coverage to the matter. We felt we had achieved something for the welfare of local youngsters.

Then just after Easter the Bishop-elect of Durham made his statement on television saying that we did not as Christians have to believe in the Virgin Birth or in the bodily resurrection of Christ from the tomb on the third day. Furthermore, he said he would welcome as a Christian someone who did not believe Christ was 'God made flesh'. Surely someone in authority would speak out against these heretical views. But, no, there seemed to be a deafening silence. I wrote to the Bishop-elect respectfully expressing my disquiet. Eventually, I received a circular reply which was completely unsatisfactory. Through our prayers in the parish we decided that if no one else appeared to be doing something then we must act. We called an emergency PCC and received enthusiastic backing for a major project. We would write to all 11,000 parochial clergy in England expressing our concern about the current moral and theological confusion in the Anglican Church. To encourage a quick response, we planned to take out a Freepost licence so that clergy could reply in the envelope provided and we would pay the postage.

With the dedicated help of our printing department and a large number of churchmembers we produced the leaflets, put them in envelopes and sorted them out into mail bags for the mass mailing. On Ascension Day we loaded my caravette with the bags and delivered them to the main sorting office. The whole project with return postage cost some £2,000 which the parish was glad to pay. It was only 7% of our outreach budget and, we felt, money well spent. One clergyman wrote back to me rather negatively saying that I must have some organisation behind me because no ordinary parish priest could afford to arrange such a project!

The replies began to come in. Two thirds of them were positive. But I received 653 negative letters from clergy. Of these 370 were fair; 189 were rude, some even vitriolic, and 94 were anonymous. Some of the anonymous ones were very sick. Quite a number simply sent the Freepost envelope back empty so we would be charged postage. I began to see more clearly just how ailing the Church of England is, both through unbiblical theology and sometimes totally unchristian attitudes as expressed in the letters.

During the first week that this was all happening I felt rather bruised and drained emotionally and my sleep was disturbed. But I just knew we had acted at the Lord's calling. One has to be mentally unbalanced to enjoy being unpopular or to be unaffected by constant personal attacks. But it was worth it. After all it was the Lord who was really being attacked, especially concerning His Virgin Birth and bodily resurrection from the tomb. The church and the national press took up the story of our protest and the setting up of 'Action for Biblical Witness to our Nation' (ABWON) as did various television companies who interviewed me. In fact, the whole thing mushroomed beyond our anticipation. We now have around 1,500 people on the mailing list—most of them clergy. I must have had some 3,000 letters recently. The most encouraging are the ones which express relief and gratitude to God that someone has taken a lead and spoken out. Those who feel that public protests are not the right approach, have little understanding of the prophetic side of Christian ministry. Nor are they really understanding the pastoral and evangelistic needs in the nation. Many Christians, clergy as well as laity, have been deeply upset and confused by the Bishop of Durham's statements and the (possibly less than accurate) Credo-poll of bishops' beliefs which claims many bishops agree with him. The fact that many bishops have so far refused to correct any inaccuracies in the poll and the mishandling of the whole situation by our overall leaders has worsened the situation. There is a tremendous pastoral need which requires meeting in as public a way as the offensive statements were. Also the confusion created in those outside the church has hindered the work of evangelism. Again this requires public correction. There will be many major battles to be won in the future. Primarily they will be won through intercession, which will be our priority in ABWON.

Some bishops hold that a person can be a Christian without believing that Jesus is 'God in the flesh'. Their statements have already been used in militant Islamic propaganda against the Divinity of Christ. Also the Church of England is greatly influenced by Freemasonry with its cultic characteristics and its 'inter-faith' description of God. These and various other activities on the Inter-Faith front are paving the way for a single world religion which would have great potential for world peace. But behind it is the spirit of Antichrist. One imminent battle, therefore, will be for the uniqueness of Christ as the Son of God and only Saviour.

ABWON is not calling for the status quo or simply for traditional Anglicanism, much as I respect some traditionalists. Rather the call is for a continuing reformation of the church according to Biblical Principles in the power of the Spirit. The law of the Church of England clearly states that Scripture is its supreme authority. The various Doctrine Reports, beloved of bishops who wish to support an excessive breadth of beliefs in the church, have, in fact, no authority whatsoever.

The time has surely come for us Anglicans—high, low, traditionalist, informal, Prayer Book Supporters, ASB users to look beyond our differences and to stand together for the truth and authority of God's Word in the church, by the power of the Spirit.

But why take such action? Why not just get on with the task of building the local church and caring for the parish? The answer is that the situation in England is urgent. The time is short. I was brought up in a context where there was great stress on expecting the Return of Christ. Sometimes, I fear, this involved an unreliable use of Scripture and trying to work out the detailed meaning of prophecies to do with the future. The result was not always helpful. In fact, sometimes it seemed like wishful thinking. I reacted against all this when I went to college. I was too concerned with the present task of the church to worry about the distant future. Besides, I wasn't sure what I believed about prophecies to do with the End Times and the Return of Christ. The various theories seemed thoroughly unconvincing.

This remained my attitude until the beginning of 1980. It was then that I began to do a series of sermons on the Old Testament. Over the next 18 months on Sunday mornings I completed a bird's eye view of the Old Testament. Each week I produced a sheet summarising a book or part of a book. For this I had to do some quite thorough study of the book concerned. I was fascinated by the historical books and I'm sure I learnt far more in the process than ever I'd done at college. Israel, its history and customs became so real to me. But it was when I reached the prophets that the study had the most profound effect on me. As I studied them and related them to history I began to react against the popular interpretation of the prophets which involves 'spiritualising' them rather than taking them literally. Of course, the prophets do use metaphorical language and it's not wrong, for example, to take a passage referring to Israel and to relate it to ourselves as a devotional thought. But I became convinced that the prophets were basically to be taken literally. Much of what they had predicted had already happened with remarkable accuracy. I found the attempts of some scholars to get round this fact, singularly unconvincing. The reality of accurately fulfilled predictive prophecy is no embarrassment to me.

I began to realise too, that when God was about to do some significant thing, he normally revealed his plan to prophets. As I said before, I cannot believe that Ephesians 4:11, which speaks of the ministry of the prophet in the church, is irrelevant to today's church. So I concluded that God wanted to reveal the future through prophecy today, mainly through insight as to how biblical prophecy is being fulfilled. I believe He will reveal a little at a time. Some prophetic passages of Scripture will only be fully understood when we approach the time for their fulfilment.

All this became real to me over a two year period and then I began to look at prophecies to do with the Return of Christ in a new light. In June 1982 I preached, for the first time ever, on Romans 9–11 about God's rejection of the Jews not being total and permanent. Rather He was going to bring about a massive turning to Christ by the Jews which would be a blessing to the world. For all the unanswered questions about details of Old Testament prophecies and the present political problems of the Middle East, I found I could do no other than see the re-establishment of Israel as a fulfilment of prophecy. This together with Israel's survival as a nation (and the Jews survival over 2,000 years of dispersion) seems miraculous. When 'Restoration', the housechurch magazine, in 1983 dismissed this understanding of Israel and referred all the Old Testament prophecies about Israel to the church, I had to disagree. I just cannot understand the Old Testament that way. If God were not going to keep his staggering promises to Israel then He would seem to me to be unfaithful. Furthermore, I would not be able to understand the survival of the Jews or the re-establishment of Israel. But if the re-establishment of Israel is a fulfilment of prophecy then we live in a very late stage before the Return of Christ.

There are other significant 'signs of the times' however. The enormous evil of nuclear armaments means we are always minutes away from oblivion. The tremendous growth in the occult and cults (false messiahs and false prophets) to which I have previously alluded is another pointer Jesus foretold. The feasibility of the Gospel being preached to the whole world through modern means of communication is another. But I believe one other sign of the times is the tremendous world wide movement of the Spirit which many claim is unparalleled in human history. It must grieve the Spirit that so many Christians have rejected God's work in renewal in recent years, as in effect I did for four years. How this must hinder God's mission to win the world. On the other hand, those who have experienced renewal and have either become inward looking or have not moved on from their initial experience must grieve Him even more. All such grieving of the Spirit requires repentance.

This brings me to the message we believe we have as a local church in Hawkwell. It can be summarised in five 'R's.

Repentance:	a definite renunciation of 'the world, the flesh and the devil' (including, of course, occult involvement) and turning to Christ through the Cross.
Renewal:	a definite experience of the power God promises us through the Holy Spirit.
Restoration:	a prayerful attempt to restore the church to Biblical principles in the power of the Spirit.

184

| *Revival*: | persistent, sacrificial prayer for thousands to be brought into the Kingdom of God by the sovereign work of the Holy Spirit. |
| *Return*: | a clear, prayerful recognition of the urgency of the time in which we live as we prepare for the Return of Christ. |

It is important to remember that the prophets not only foretold the future. They spoke into the evils of their society, warned of judgment and called for repentance. I believe England is heading for God's judgment. Perhaps the most privileged nation as far as Christian heritage is concerned, we are an increasingly godless, immoral and violent people. But judgment always begins at the household of God. As the national church, we Anglicans are first in line for it. The fairly general decline in our church as proved by recent statistics, is part of it. Public denials of vital truths about Christ, especially when tolerated by the church, can only hasten it. But I believe this need not be a final judgment. If we heed the warning signs and put our house in order we, and more to the point, the nation, can be saved.

Appendix: Our Vision of the Nature and Mission of the Local Church

We aim:

1. To be wholeheartedly committed to Christ as Saviour and Lord. (John 20:31; Rom.10:9).

2. To be baptised in water and confirmed. (Acts 19:5–6).

3. To read the Bible regularly, accepting its authority and acting on it by the power of the Holy Spirit so that the church may be made more true to the Bible under the Lordship of Christ. (2 Timothy 3:16–17).

4. To seek personally and to encourage others to seek the release of the Baptism of the Holy Spirit as a definite experience, and daily filling with the Spirit, so that our eyes may be open fully to our riches in Christ and the vision God is revealing. (Acts 2:17, 38–39)

5. To seek personally and to encourage others to seek security in God (which is faith) not in our own understanding, efforts, other people, material things, circumstances, or traditional patterns. (Proverbs 28:26; Jeremiah 17:5–8; I Timothy 6:17).

186

6. To seek personally and to encourage others to seek that spiritual 'brokenness' before God, so that our wills are submitted to His and His will is all that matters. (Matthew 7:21–23). To aim at holiness of life based on the fruit of the Spirit, and to seek for inner healing as necessary, so that there are no barriers to spiritual progress (e.g. fear of commitment, other people, circumstances or the future.) (Psalm 118:6–9; Matthew 6:25–34).

7. To join regularly in worship and to encourage the building of a worshipping community which will know regularly what it is to adore God, being 'lost in wonder, love and praise' and to express this worship fully. (Psalm 100).

8. To learn to intercede for others and to listen often in prayer for God's specific guidance and developing vision for the future. (Romans 8:26–27; Ephesians 6:18; Isaiah 30:15,18,21).

9. To seek the church's guidance to find our gifts and use them. To encourage the discovery of every member's spiritual gifts and ministries so that all the gifts of the Spirit will operate in the church; that people will only be doing the things which the leaders in the church have helped them to recognise or confirmed that God has called them to and gifted them for. (Ephesians 4:11–16; I Corinthians 12).

10. To be deeply committed personally and to encourage others to be deeply committed to the church as a community, not each 'doing his or her own thing' in the rebellious spirit of the age; but aiming to achieve a unity of heart and mind in which the church moves enthusiasti-

187

cally as one in obedience to God so that the world may believe. (Eph.6:21; John 17:21–23).

To accept the authority of the elders and other leaders, respecting them, obeying them in teaching and advice that the Bible clearly supports and in matters which affect the church. (1 Thess.5:12–13; Hebrews 13—17)

To be completely loyal to one another—keeping confidences, defending one another against negative criticism, not being judgmental or jumping to conclusions about each other. (Galatians 5:13–15; Colossians 3:12–15).

To be open and honest with one another, including giving and receiving prayerful encouragement and correction and putting right any gossip or negative criticism in each other. (Matthew 18:15–17; Galatians 6:1–2; Ephesians 4:15; Titus 3:1–2; Titus 3:10–11; James 5:19–20).

To encourage the sharing of important personal issues with others, particularly with leaders, confidentially, for prayer and guidance before making a decision. (Prov.12:15; 1 Peter 5:5).

To share material things with one another, to give at least a tenth of income to God and to ensure a fellow member is not left in serious financial need. (Leviticus 27:30; Malachi 3:8–10; Matthew 5:42; 2 Cor.8:13–15; 9:6–8; 1 John 3:17).

To encourage the church to become more caring by accepting pastoral responsibility being given to the many rather than the few, so that the church may become a truly loving community and a place where God's healing power will be operating in obvious ways. (Matthew 4:18; Ephesians 4:16)

To base family life and to encourage others to base their

188

family life on the Biblical principles of love, fellowship, submission and discipline, and to see that single and widowed members are included in families. (Ephesians 5:22–6:4).

To be involved regularly in one of the fellowship groups organised by the church. (Acts 2:42, 46, 47; Hebrews 10:24–25).

11. To support the church as it invades 'the gates of Hell', enabling Christians to recognise and resist the enemy; bringing deliverance to people from bondage to sin, weakness, habit and Satan; by evangelism with 'signs following'; by giving prophetic messages from the Lord to the world. (Matthew 16:18–19; 28:18–20; Mark 16:17–18; Amos 3:7–8; Ezekiel 3:16–18; Revelation 1:3).

12. To support the church as it stresses the urgency of the church's mission to the world in the light of the Return of Christ, working with fellowships who share this vision and encouraging other fellowships into the vision. (Acts 10:42; 1 Timothy 4:1–2; Hebrews 10:24–25).

Other Marshall Pickering Paperbacks

THROUGH DAVID'S PSALMS

Derek Prince

Derek Prince, internationally known Bible teacher and scholar, draws on his understanding of the Hebrew language and culture, and a comprehensive knowledge of Scripture, to present 101 meditations from the Psalms.
Each of these practical and enriching meditations is based on a specific passage and concludes with a faith response. They can be used either for personal meditation or for family devotions. They are intended for all those who want their lives enriched or who seek comfort and encouragement from the Scriptures.

LOVING GOD

Charles Colson

Loving God is the very purpose of the believer's life, the vocation for which he is made. However loving God is not easy and most people have given little real thought to what the greatest commandment really means.
Many books have been written on the individual subjects of repentence, Bible study, prayer, outreach, evangelism, holiness and other elements of the Christian life. In **Loving God**, Charles Colson draws all these elements together to look at the entire process of growing up as a Christian.
Combining vivid illustrations with straightforward exposition he shows how to live out the Christian faith in our daily lives. **Loving God** provides a real challenge to deeper commitment and points the way towards greater maturity.

OUT OF THE MELTING POT

Bob Gordon

Faith does not operate in a vacuum, it operates in human lives. God wants your life to be a crucible of faith.
Bob Gordon draws together Biblical principles and personal experience to provide valuable insights into this key area. Particular reference is made to the lessons he leant recently as God provided £600,000 to buy Roffey Place Christian Training Centre.
Out of the Melting Pot is Bob Gordon's powerful testimony to the work of God today and a profound challenge to shallow views of faith.

BILLY GRAHAM

John Pollock

By any reckoning, Billy Graham is one of the major religious figures of the twentieth-century.
John Pollock tells the highlights of the Billy Graham story briefly and vividly for the general reader. Using existing material and brand new information the story is taken right up the eve of Mission England.
This is an authoritative biography which pays special attention to the recent developments in Dr. Graham's life and ministry. Fully endorsed by Billy Graham himself, the book is full of fascinating new insights into the man and his mission.

". . . fascinating reading"

London Bible College Review

". . . a difficult book to put down"

Church of England Newspaper

THE TORN VEIL

Sister Gulshan and Thelma Sangster

Gulshan Fatima was brought up in a Muslim Sayed family according to the orthodox Islamic code of the Shias.

Suffering from a crippling paralysis she travelled to England in search of medical help. Although unsuccessful in medical terms, this trip marked the beginning of a spiritual awakening that led ultimately to her conversion to Christianity.

Gulshan and her father also travelled to Mecca in the hope that God would heal her, but that trip too was of no avail. However, Gulshan was not detered. She relentlessly pursued God and He faithfully answered her prayers. Her conversion, when it came, was dramatic and brought with a miraculous healing.

The Torn Veil is Sister Gulshan's thrilling testimony to the power of God which can break through every barrier.

NOW I CALL HIM BROTHER

Alec Smith

Alec Smith, son of Ian Smith the rebel Prime Minister of Rhodesia whose Unilateral Declaration of Independence plunged his country into twelve years of bloody racial war, has written his own story of those years

The story of his life takes him from early years of rebellion against his role as 'Ian Smith's son' through his youth as a drop-out, hippy and drug peddler into the Rhodesian forces.

A dramatic Christian conversion experience at the height of the civil war transformed his life and led to the passionate conviction to see reconciliation and peace in a deeply divided country.

What follows is a thrilling account of how God can take a dedicated life and help to change the course of history.

HOW TO MANAGE PRESSURE
Before Pressure Manages You

Tim LaHaye

Pressure is unavoidable. Everyone faces pressure in some area of their life. Even as you read this, you may be aware of pressures in your life that cause worry and tension and hinder your sense of well being.

The good news of this book is that there is a way to handle pressure so that it can become a creative rather than destructive force.

Tim LaHaye offers insights that will enable you to relieve stress and to live a more satisfying life amidst those everyday pressures.

LOVE LIFE FOR EVERY MARRIED COUPLE

Dr E. Wheat

Dr Wheat, a physician and therapist, has helped thousands of troubled couples improve their love lives and build happier marriages with his unique counselling methods. In **Love Life for Every Married Couple,** Dr Wheat explores marital conflict in a straightforward manner, focusing on the reasons why couples experience frustration and unhappiness in their love lives.

"Dr Wheat has revealed, again, his unique talent for identifying the critical issues in family living, and then offering wise counsel and loving support to those who hurt ... I recommend Love Life to those who want a better marriage."
                                                                Dr James Dobson

If you wish to receive *regular information* about *new books*, please send your name and address to:

London Bible Warehouse
PO Box 123
Basingstoke
Hants RG23 7NL

Name...

Address ....

....

....

....

I am especially interested in:
☐ Biographies
☐ Fiction
☐ Christian living
☐ Issue related books
☐ Academic books
☐ Bible study aids
☐ Children's books
☐ Music
☐ Other subjects

P.S. If you have ideas for new Christian Books or other products, please write to us too!